# Scott Foresman

Reading

Grade 4

# Skills Tests
# Teacher's Manual

## Scott Foresman

**Editorial Offices:** Glenview, Illinois • New York, New York
**Sales Offices:** Reading, Massachusetts • Duluth, Georgia • Glenview, Illinois
Carrollton, Texas • Menlo Park, California

**Editorial Offices**
Glenview, Illinois • New York, New York

**Sales Offices**
Reading, Massachusetts • Duluth, Georgia • Glenview, Illinois
Carrollton, Texas • Menlo Park, California

ISBN 0-673-62455-2

3 4 5 6 7 8 9 10-BW-06 05 04 03 02 01

# CONTENTS

Overview . . . . . . . . . . . . . . . . . . . . . . . . . . . . . . . . . . . . . . . T1

Using These Tests . . . . . . . . . . . . . . . . . . . . . . . . . . . . . . . . T2

Administering the Tests . . . . . . . . . . . . . . . . . . . . . . . . . . T3

Scoring the Tests . . . . . . . . . . . . . . . . . . . . . . . . . . . . . . . . T4

Evaluation Charts . . . . . . . . . . . . . . . . . . . . . . . . . . . . . . .T10

SKILLS TESTS . . . . . . . . . . . . . . . . . . . . . . . . . . . . . . . . . . . .1
    Unit 1
    Unit 2
    Unit 3
    Unit 4
    Unit 5
    Unit 6
    End-of-Year

Answer Sheets . . . . . . . . . . . . . . . . . . . . . . . . . . . . . . . . . .T18

Answer Keys . . . . . . . . . . . . . . . . . . . . . . . . . . . . . . . . . . .T20

# OVERVIEW

*Scott Foresman Reading* provides a wide array of formal tests and classroom assessments to support instruction. Formal assessments include the following:

- Placement Tests
- Selection Tests
- Unit Skills Tests and End-of-Year Test
- Unit Benchmark Tests and End-of-Year Test

This Teacher's Manual provides information for administering the Skills Tests, scoring the tests, and interpreting the results. Detailed information about other assessment materials and procedures may be found in the *Assessment Handbook*.

## Description of the Skills Tests

In Grade 4, there are six Unit Skills Tests—one for each unit—and an End-of-Year Test. The Unit Skills Tests are designed to measure a student's progress based on specific skills taught in each unit and to help you identify a student's specific strengths and weaknesses. Each Unit Skills Test has two parts. Each of these parts has two or three subtests.

The **Reading** part includes the following subtests:

- a Comprehension subtest that measures comprehension skills, vocabulary strategies, and literary genres and skills in relation to literature selections, including fiction, poetry, drama, nonfiction, and "functional" texts (posters, want ads, invitations, and the like)

- a Word Analysis subtest that measures word study and phonics skills taught in the unit (beginning in Unit 3)

The **Writing/Study Skills** part includes the following subtests:

- a Writing/Grammar subtest that measures grammar, usage, and mechanics skills taught in the unit, generally in the context of a written text

- a Writing prompt based on the targeted type of writing taught in the writing process activity in the unit

- a Study Skills subtest that measures skills taught in the unit, often in the context of a writing project or activity

The Unit Skills Tests are designed so that you may determine a separate score for each skill in Reading: Comprehension; a separate score for each subtest; and a total test score. In Reading: Comprehension, each skill is tested by at least four items. The Word Analysis, Writing/Grammar, and Study Skills subtest have a total of five to ten items each. All Skills Test questions are multiple-choice items, except for the Writing prompt.

The End-of-Year Skills Test follows the same design as the Unit Skills Test, but it is a longer test, and it measures selected skills from all six units taught during the year. It is designed to provide a score for each subtest and a total test score.

The design of the Skills Tests is the result of a two-year development effort, which included the administration of selected tests in a field tryout in the spring of 1998. Results from that field tryout, which involved a representative sample of students across the United States, were used to help refine the tests and ensure an appropriate level of difficulty.

# USING THESE TESTS

The Skills Tests are designed for group administration in two or more sittings. Each Unit Skills Test includes 40–45 test items organized in five subtests. These tests are not intended to be timed. We recommend allowing ample time for all students to complete the tests at their own rates. However, for the purposes of scheduling and planning, the chart below shows the number of items in each test and the estimated amount of time required to complete each section.

| Unit Skills Test: Units 1–6 | | |
| --- | --- | --- |
| Subtest | Number of Items | Estimated Time |
| Reading: Comprehension | 24–25 | 30 minutes |
| Reading: Word Analysis | 6 | 5 minutes |
| Writing/Grammar | 5–6 | 5 minutes |
| Writing | 1 Writing prompt | 20–30 minutes |
| Study Skills | 5–10 | 5–10 minutes |

| End-of-Year Skills Test | | |
| --- | --- | --- |
| Subtest | Number of Items | Estimated Time |
| Reading: Comprehension | 30 | 45 minutes |
| Reading: Word Analysis | 10 | 10 minutes |
| Writing/Grammar | 10 | 10 minutes |
| Writing | 1 Writing prompt | 20–30 minutes |
| Study Skills | 10 | 10 minutes |

Each Unit Skills Test has four reading selections. The End-of-Year Skills Test has five reading selections.

# ADMINISTERING THE TESTS

For each test in Grade 4, all questions except the Writing prompt are multiple-choice items with four answer choices (labeled A, B, C, D or F, G, H, J in alternating items).

## Before you administer a test . . .

Review the test to familiarize yourself with the directions and the types of questions. Distribute a test to each student and make sure students have pencils for marking and writing their responses. Have students write their names on the front of the test and respond directly on the test pages by marking the letter for each answer. For the writing prompt, students should write their responses on the lined pages provided.

If you want students to take tests using an answer sheet, use the reproducible forms on pages T18–19. Make a copy of the appropriate page—for the Unit Skills Test or End-of-Year Skills Test—and have students fill in the name and date lines at the top. (For the Unit Skills Test, have them fill in the unit number as well.) Students should mark their answers by filling in the correct bubbles. (They will need to use separate lined paper for responding to the writing prompt.)

## When you are ready to administer a test . . .

Students should read all test directions and answer the questions independently.

For each test that you administer, decide how many sessions to schedule. This decision will depend mainly on class schedules and how much testing your students can manage successfully in one session. If you choose to administer a Unit Skills Test in two sessions, you may want to test Reading in one session and Writing and Study Skills in another, as shown below:

| Test Administration Plan: Two Sessions | |
| --- | --- |
| 1. Reading: Comprehension<br>　 Reading: Word Analysis | 2. Writing/Grammar<br>　 Writing prompt<br>　 Study Skills |
| Time: 30–40 minutes | Time: 45–50 minutes |

The directions for administering tests are designed to have students stop at the end of each subtest. Students will see a STOP sign at the bottom of the last page in each section. (If you want students to complete more than one subtest in a sitting, tell them which pages to complete before they stop.)

To begin a test, read the general directions below:

General Directions
**This is a test about reading and writing. Each question in the Reading section has four answer choices. Choose the best answer to each question and mark the letter for your answer. In the Writing section, you will answer some questions about language and you will respond to a writing prompt by writing a short composition.**

Tell students which part(s) of the test they will be expected to complete in each session and how much time they have. Then direct students to open their tests, read the directions, and answer the questions.

## After testing . . .

Directions for scoring the tests follow. Answer Keys for all tests are in the back of this Teacher's Manual.

# SCORING THE TESTS

All Skills Tests are intended to be scored by subtest and total test. In the Unit Tests, the Reading: Comprehension subtest may also be scored by skill. (For a sample, see page T5.)

A total score for the Reading part of the test can be determined by adding together the scores for Reading: Comprehension and Reading: Word Analysis.

A score for the total test can be determined by adding together the numbers for all subtests except the Writing prompt, which is scored separately.

## Scoring Multiple-Choice Items

Each multiple-choice item has four answer choices (A, B, C, D or F, G, H, J). Referring to the Answer Key for the test, mark each multiple-choice item correct or incorrect.

## Scoring the Writing Activity

The Writing activity requires students to produce a written response. To evaluate the students' responses, read the writing prompt. Then, to score a response, review the Scoring Guide provided in the Answer Key. Read the student's writing and score it on a scale of 1 to 4, based on the criteria described in the Answer Key.

The criteria provided in each Scoring Guide are based on the key features of specific kinds of writing—as they have been taught in the writing process activities. The 4-point scale reflects the general levels of performance defined below; these levels are defined more specifically for each Writing activity.

### Scoring Guides: 4-Point Scale

#### 4 Exemplary

An "exemplary" response includes all the key features required for the specific type of writing. Errors in grammar, usage, and mechanics are minimal and do not prevent understanding.

#### 3 Competent

A "competent" response includes most of the key features required for the specific type of writing. It may include a few errors in grammar, usage, and mechanics, but they do not prevent understanding.

#### 2 Developing

A "developing" response includes some key features required for the specific type of writing. It may include several errors in grammar, usage, and mechanics, which may prevent understanding.

#### 1 Emerging

An "emerging" response needs improvement. It does not include key features required for the specific type of writing. Errors in grammar, usage, and mechanics prevent understanding.

# Using an Evaluation Chart

On pages T10–T16 are seven Evaluation Charts: one for each Unit Skills Test and one for the End-of-Year Skills Test. On page T17 is a Class Record Chart for recording test scores from all students.

**To score a Skills Test using an Evaluation Chart, we recommend the following procedure:**

1. Make a copy of the appropriate Evaluation Chart for each student.
2. Refer to the Answer Key for the test you are scoring.
3. For multiple-choice questions, mark the response to each question correct or incorrect. On the Evaluation Chart, circle the question number for each item answered correctly. Draw an X through the number of each question answered incorrectly.
4. To find the total score for a subtest, skill, or total test, add the number of items answered correctly.
5. To determine a percentage score for the number of items answered correctly—by subtest, by skill, or by total test—use one of the tables on pages T6–T7.

The sample below shows scoring for each Reading: Comprehension skill included in one Unit Skills Test (Cause and effect, Author's viewpoint, and so on), as well as a total score for the Comprehension subtest, one for the Word Analysis subtest, and one for the entire Reading part of the test.

| SUBTEST<br>Skill/Item Numbers | | | | | | | Number<br>Correct | % |
|---|---|---|---|---|---|---|---|---|
| **READING: Comprehension** | | | | | | | | |
| Cause and effect | ① | ✗ | ⑦ | ⑬ | | | 3/4 | 75% |
| Author's viewpoint | ③ | ④ | ✗ | ⑱ | | | 3/4 | 75% |
| Graphic sources | ⑧ | ⑨ | ✗ | ㉒ | | | 3/4 | 75% |
| Steps in a process | ⑭ | ✗ | ✗ | ㉓ | | | 2/4 | 50% |
| Literary genre, similes, metaphor | ✗ | ⑫ | ⑯ | ㉔ | | | 3/4 | 75% |
| Vocabulary: Multiple-meaning words | ⑤ | ⑪ | ⑮ | ㉑ | | | 4/4 | 100% |
| **Total Comprehension** | | | | | | | 18/24 | 75% |
| **READING: Word Analysis** | | | | | | | | |
| Prefixes | ✗ | ㉖ | ㉗ | ✗ | ㉙ | ㉚ | 4/6 | 67% |
| **TOTAL READING** | | | | | | | 22/30 | 73% |

6. For the Writing activity, review the Scoring Guide provided in the Answer Key. Then read the student's writing and score it on a scale of 1 to 4, based on the criteria described in the Key.
7. Mark the student's score for writing on the Evaluation Chart. Add any notes or observations about the writing that may be helpful to you and the student in later instruction.

# Percentage Scores

Tables 1 and 2 that follow show percentage scores for Unit Skills Tests—by subtest and by skill, respectively. Table 3 shows percentage scores for the End-of-Year Test.

To find a percentage score by subtest in Table 1, locate the number of items answered correctly in the "Number Correct" column. Then go across to the column for the subtest you are scoring. For example, a student who answers 18 of 24 items correctly in Reading: Comprehension has achieved a percentage score of 75%. (Note that the number of items in Comprehension varies from 24 to 25 in different units, the number of items in Writing/Grammar varies from 5 to 6, and the number of items in Study Skills varies from 5 to 10.)

## Table 1. Percentage Scores for Subtests in the Unit Skills Tests

| Number Correct | Reading: Comprehension 24 | Reading: Comprehension 25 | Reading: Word Analysis | TOTAL READING | Writing/ Grammar 5 | Writing/ Grammar 6 | Study Skills 5 | Study Skills 10 |
|---|---|---|---|---|---|---|---|---|
| 1 | 4% | 4% | 17% | 3% | 20% | 17% | 20% | 10% |
| 2 | 8% | 8% | 33% | 7% | 40% | 33% | 40% | 20% |
| 3 | 13% | 12% | 50% | 10% | 60% | 50% | 60% | 30% |
| 4 | 17% | 16% | 67% | 13% | 80% | 67% | 80% | 40% |
| 5 | 21% | 20% | 83% | 17% | 100% | 83% | 100% | 50% |
| 6 | 25% | 24% | 100% | 20% | | 100% | | 60% |
| 7 | 29% | 28% | | 23% | | | | 70% |
| 8 | 33% | 32% | | 27% | | | | 80% |
| 9 | 38% | 36% | | 30% | | | | 90% |
| 10 | 42% | 40% | | 33% | | | | 100% |
| 11 | 46% | 44% | | 37% | | | | |
| 12 | 50% | 48% | | 40% | | | | |
| 13 | 54% | 52% | | 43% | | | | |
| 14 | 58% | 56% | | 47% | | | | |
| 15 | 63% | 60% | | 50% | | | | |
| 16 | 67% | 64% | | 53% | | | | |
| 17 | 71% | 68% | | 57% | | | | |
| 18 | 75% | 72% | | 60% | | | | |
| 19 | 79% | 76% | | 63% | | | | |
| 20 | 83% | 80% | | 67% | | | | |
| 21 | 88% | 84% | | 70% | | | | |
| 22 | 92% | 88% | | 73% | | | | |
| 23 | 96% | 92% | | 77% | | | | |
| 24 | 100% | 96% | | 80% | | | | |
| 25 | | 100% | | 83% | | | | |
| 26 | | | | 87% | | | | |
| 27 | | | | 90% | | | | |
| 28 | | | | 93% | | | | |
| 29 | | | | 97% | | | | |
| 30 | | | | 100% | | | | |

# Table 2. Percentage Scores for Individual Skills in the Unit Skills Tests

| Number Correct | Skill (4 items) | Skill (5 items) |
|---|---|---|
| 1 | 25% | 20% |
| 2 | 50% | 40% |
| 3 | 75% | 60% |
| 4 | 100% | 80% |
| 5 | | 100% |

To find a percentage score by skill in Table 2, locate the number of items answered correctly in the "Number Correct" column. Then go across to the column for the number of items per skill (which may be 4 or 5, depending on the skill). For example, a student who answers 3 of 4 items correctly for a skill measured by 4 items has achieved a percentage score of 75%.

# Table 3. Percentage Scores by Subtest for End-of-Year Skills Test

| Number Correct | Reading: Comprehension | Word Analysis, Writing/Grammar, or Study Skills |
|---|---|---|
| 1 | 4% | 10% |
| 2 | 8% | 20% |
| 3 | 12% | 30% |
| 4 | 16% | 40% |
| 5 | 20% | 50% |
| 6 | 24% | 60% |
| 7 | 28% | 70% |
| 8 | 32% | 80% |
| 9 | 36% | 90% |
| 10 | 40% | 100% |
| 11 | 44% | |
| 12 | 48% | |
| 13 | 52% | |
| 14 | 56% | |
| 15 | 60% | |
| 16 | 64% | |
| 17 | 68% | |
| 18 | 72% | |
| 19 | 76% | |
| 20 | 80% | |
| 21 | 84% | |
| 22 | 88% | |
| 23 | 92% | |
| 24 | 96% | |
| 25 | 100% | |

To find a percentage score by subtest in Table 3, locate the number of items answered correctly in the "Number Correct" column. Then go across to the column for the subtest you are scoring. For example, a student who answers 24 of 30 items correctly in Reading: Comprehension has achieved a percentage score of 80%.

To determine the percentage score for a total test, find the total number of items answered correctly. Divide the total number correct by the total number of items on the test. For example, the Unit 1 Skills Test has a total of 40 multiple-choice items. Suppose a student answers a total of 28 items correctly: $28 \div 40 = 0.70$, or 70%.

# Interpreting Test Results

A student's score on the Skills Test provides only one look at a student's developmental progress and should be interpreted in conjunction with other assessments and the teacher's observations. However, a low score on one or more parts of the Skills Test probably indicates a need for closer review of the student's performance and perhaps additional instruction.

For these Skills Tests, we recommend a passing score of at least 70% on each subtest (Reading: Comprehension; Reading: Word Analysis; Writing/Grammar; and Study Skills) and, for a response to the Writing prompt, a score of at least 2 on the 4-point scale. If you score the Reading: Comprehension subtest by skill, students should achieve a score of at least 70% for each skill. (The Evaluation Chart for each Unit Skills Test lists the test items by skill.)

For a student who does not achieve these scores, you may want to review the student's test more carefully to identify which items the student answered incorrectly and to determine skills or specific areas in which the student needs additional help. The chart below is intended to provide guidelines for making instructional decisions based on Skills Test scores. Unless otherwise specified, all activities listed may be found in the Teacher's Edition.

## Interpreting Test Scores

| | |
|---|---|
| **Students who score *90% or higher* on each subtest and on each skill . . .** | **. . . need to be challenged.**<br><br>An instructional plan might include:<br><br>• Meeting Diverse Needs: Challenge activities to enhance the skills of students who perform at high levels<br><br>• Leveled Readers Set C (challenge) to provide experience with target comprehension skills at a more challenging reading level |
| **Students who score *70%–89%* on each subtest and on each skill . . .** | **. . . need additional instructional support.**<br><br>An instructional plan might include:<br><br>• "If . . . then . . ." suggestions to guide instruction as indicated<br><br>• Review skill lessons to maintain previously introduced phonics and comprehension skills<br><br>• Daily Word Routines to provide quick phonics, vocabulary, and language arts practice<br><br>• Leveled Readers Set B (easy/average) to reinforce comprehension skills and practice tested words |

| Students who score *below 70%* on any subtest *or* on any skill . . . | . . . need frequent teacher support and may need intervention. |
|---|---|
| | An instructional plan might include: |
| | • Ongoing Assessment: "If . . . then . . ." suggestions to guide instruction for students as they experience difficulty |
| | • Part 3 Comprehension lesson, which reteaches the target skill by breaking it into its component parts and applying it to less demanding text |
| | • Skills in Context to provide additional skill instruction and modeling |
| | • Meeting Diverse Needs: Intervention activities to provide intervention in oral language, comprehension, word study, and fluency |
| | • Leveled Readers Set A (easy) and Set B (easy/average) to reinforce comprehension skills and practice tested words |

A student who scores low on one skill but reasonably well on the total subtest may need special attention in one or more areas. For example, a student might answer 18 of 24 Reading items correctly for a subtest score of 75%. However, within that subtest, the student may have answered incorrectly on all four test items measuring "Main idea," which may indicate a need for additional help in this area.

For any student whose Skills Test scores are not clearly definitive, we recommend administering additional assessments, such as the Individual Reading Inventory. For more information about other assessments, refer to the *Assessment Handbook*.

**Grading.** If you would like more information on how to use a writing assessment scale for determining grades, refer to the "Grading Writing" section of the *Assessment Handbook*.

Student Name _____ Date _____

| SUBTEST<br>Skill/Item Numbers | | | | | | Number Correct | % |
|---|---|---|---|---|---|---|---|
| **READING: Comprehension** | | | | | | | |
| Setting | | 1 | 11 | 15 | 19 | | |
| Character | | 2 | 8 | 13 | 23 | | |
| Sequence | | 4 | 7 | 14 | 22 | | |
| Author's purpose | | 6 | 12 | 17 | 24 | | |
| Literary genre and point of view | 3 | 10 | 18 | 20 | 25 | | |
| Vocabulary: Unfamiliar words | | 5 | 9 | 16 | 21 | | |
| **TOTAL READING** | | | | | | | |
| **WRITING/GRAMMAR** | | | | | | | |
| Sentences | 1 | 2 | 3 | 4 | 5 | | |
| **WRITING** | | | | | | | |
| Personal Narrative | | 1 | 2 | 3 | 4 | | |
| **STUDY SKILLS** | | | | | | | |
| Textbook, Parts of a book, | 1 | 2 | 3 | 4 | 5 | | |
| Outlining | 6 | 7 | 8 | 9 | 10 | | |
| **TOTAL TEST (all multiple-choice items)** | | | | | | | |

Student Name _____ Date _____

| SUBTEST<br>Skill/Item Numbers | | | | | | | Number<br>Correct | % |
|---|---|---|---|---|---|---|---|---|
| **READING: Comprehension** | | | | | | | | |
| Cause and Effect | | | 1 | 7 | 16 | 19 | | |
| Context Clues | | | 2 | 11 | 20 | 24 | | |
| Visualizing | | | 3 | 13 | 14 | 23 | | |
| Theme | | | 4 | 5 | 9 | 10 | | |
| Literary genre, imagery and sensory words | | 12 | 15 | 17 | 21 | | | |
| Vocabulary: Synonyms | | | 6 | 8 | 18 | 22 | | |
| **TOTAL READING** | | | | | | | | |
| **WRITING/GRAMMAR** | | | | | | | | |
| Nouns | 1 | 2 | 3 | 4 | 5 | 6 | | |
| **WRITING** | | | | | | | | |
| Description | | | 1 | 2 | 3 | 4 | | |
| **STUDY SKILLS** | | | | | | | | |
| Newspapers/Magazines/Periodicals, | 1 | 2 | 3 | 4 | 5 | | | |
| Chart/Table, Encyclopedia | | 6 | 7 | 8 | 9 | 10 | | |
| **TOTAL TEST (all multiple-choice items)** | | | | | | | | |

# Evaluation Chart

Student Name _____ Date _____

| SUBTEST<br>Skill/Item Numbers | | | | | | Number<br>Correct | % |
|---|---|---|---|---|---|---|---|
| **READING: Comprehension** | | | | | | | |
| Drawing conclusions | 3 | 5 | 14 | 19 | | | |
| Character | 7 | 8 | 10 | 11 | | | |
| Generalizing | 4 | 9 | 13 | 24 | | | |
| Making judgments | 1 | 15 | 16 | 20 | | | |
| Literary genre, similes, metaphors | 6 | 12 | 17 | 23 | | | |
| Vocabulary: Homophones | 2 | 18 | 21 | 22 | | | |
| **Total Comprehension** | | | | | | | |
| **READING: Word Analysis** | | | | | | | |
| Regular plurals 25 26 | 27 | 28 | 29 | 30 | | | |
| **TOTAL READING** | | | | | | | |
| **WRITING/GRAMMAR** | | | | | | | |
| Verbs | 1 | 2 | 3 | 4 | 5 | | |
| **WRITING** | | | | | | | |
| Comparison/Contrast Essay, | | 1 | 2 | 3 | 4 | | |
| **STUDY SKILLS** | | | | | | | |
| Card catalog/Library database,<br>Schedule | 1 | 2 | 3 | 4 | 5 | | |
| **TOTAL TEST (all multiple-choice items)** | | | | | | | |

# Evaluation Chart

Student Name _____ Date _____

| SUBTEST<br>**Skill/Item Numbers** | | | | | | | Number<br>Correct | % |
|---|---|---|---|---|---|---|---|---|
| **READING: Comprehension** | | | | | | | | |
| Plot | | | 1 | 13 | 14 | 20 | | |
| Comparing and contrasting | | | 2 | 8 | 16 | 22 | | |
| Predicting | | | 3 | 7 | 15 | 21 | | |
| Paraphrasing | | | 6 | 12 | 18 | 24 | | |
| Literary genre and idioms | | | 4 | 9 | 17 | 19 | | |
| Vocabulary: Antonyms | | | 5 | 10 | 11 | 23 | | |
| **Total Comprehension** | | | | | | | | |
| **READING: Word Analysis** | | | | | | | | |
| Inflected forms with −*es*;<br>Suffixes | 25 | 26 | 27 | 28 | 29 | 30 | | |
| **TOTAL READING** | | | | | | | | |
| **WRITING/GRAMMAR** | | | | | | | | |
| Adjectives, Adverbs | | 1 | 2 | 3 | 4 | 5 | | |
| **WRITING** | | | | | | | | |
| How-To Report | | | 1 | 2 | 3 | 4 | | |
| **STUDY SKILLS** | | | | | | | | |
| Evaluating reference sources, | | 1 | 2 | 3 | 4 | 5 | | |
| Order form, Alphabetical | | 6 | 7 | 8 | 9 | 10 | | |
| order, Time line | | | | | | | | |
| **TOTAL TEST (all multiple-choice items)** | | | | | | | | |

Student Name _____ Date _____

| SUBTEST<br>Skill/Item Numbers | | | | | | | Number<br>Correct | % |
|---|---|---|---|---|---|---|---|---|
| **READING: Comprehension** | | | | | | | | |
| Summarizing | | 1 | 7 | 14 | 19 | | | |
| Text Structure | | 6 | 8 | 11 | 18 | | | |
| Graphic Sources | | 4 | 5 | 10 | 16 | | | |
| Generalizing | | 3 | 12 | 17 | 23 | | | |
| Literary genre, similes, metaphors | | 2 | 9 | 13 | 21 | | | |
| Vocabulary: Multiple-meaning words | | 15 | 20 | 22 | 24 | | | |
| **Total Comprehension** | | | | | | | | |
| **READING: Word Analysis** | | | | | | | | |
| Prefixes, plural possessives, syllabication | 25 | 26 | 27 | 28 | 29 | 30 | | |
| **TOTAL READING** | | | | | | | | |
| **WRITING/GRAMMAR** | | | | | | | | |
| Pronouns, Prepositions, Conjunctions | 1 | 2 | 3 | 4 | 5 | | | |
| **WRITING** | | | | | | | | |
| Research Report | | 1 | 2 | 3 | 4 | | | |
| **STUDY SKILLS** | | | | | | | | |
| Graphs, Atlas/Maps | 1 | 2 | 3 | 4 | 5 | | | |
| **TOTAL TEST (all multiple-choice items)** | | | | | | | | |

Student Name _____ Date _____

| SUBTEST<br>Skill/Item Numbers | | | | | | | Number<br>Correct | % |
|---|---|---|---|---|---|---|---|---|
| **READING: Comprehension** | | | | | | | | |
| Main idea and supporting details | | 1 | 2 | 7 | 13 | | | |
| Steps in a process | | 4 | 15 | 19 | 21 | | | |
| Author's purpose | | 3 | 11 | 17 | 22 | | | |
| Fact and opinion | | 6 | 8 | 10 | 14 | | | |
| Literary genre and flashback | | 5 | 9 | 16 | 23 | | | |
| Vocabulary: Unfamiliar words | | 12 | 18 | 20 | 24 | | | |
| **Total Comprehension** | | | | | | | | |
| **READING: Word Analysis** | | | | | | | | |
| Irregular plurals; word building and sound changes | 25 | 26 | 27 | 28 | 29 | 30 | | |
| **TOTAL READING** | | | | | | | | |
| **WRITING/GRAMMAR** | | | | | | | | |
| Punctuation | 1 | 2 | 3 | 4 | 5 | | | |
| **WRITING** | | | | | | | | |
| Persuasive Argument | | 1 | 2 | 3 | 4 | | | |
| **STUDY SKILLS** | | | | | | | | |
| Poster/Advertisement, Dictionary | 1 | 2 | 3 | 4 | 5 | | | |
| **TOTAL TEST (all multiple-choice items)** | | | | | | | | |

# Evaluation Chart                                    End-of-Year Skills Test

Student Name _____ Date _____

| SUBTEST<br>**Skill/Item Numbers** | | | | | Number<br>Correct | % |
|---|---|---|---|---|---|---|
| **READING: Comprehension** | | | | | | |
| 1 | 7 | 13 | 19 | 25 | | |
| 2 | 8 | 14 | 20 | 26 | | |
| 3 | 9 | 15 | 21 | 27 | | |
| 4 | 10 | 16 | 22 | 28 | | |
| 5 | 11 | 17 | 23 | 29 | | |
| 6 | 12 | 18 | 24 | 30 | | |
| **READING: Word Analysis** | | | | | | |
| 1 | 3 | 5 | 7 | 9 | | |
| 2 | 4 | 6 | 8 | 10 | | |
| **TOTAL READING** | | | | | | |
| **WRITING/GRAMMAR** | | | | | | |
| 1 | 3 | 5 | 7 | 9 | | |
| 2 | 4 | 6 | 8 | 10 | | |
| **WRITING** | | | | | | |
| Comparison/Contrast Essay | | | | | | |
| 1 | 2 | 3 | 4 | | | |
| **STUDY SKILLS** | | | | | | |
| 1 | 3 | 5 | 7 | 9 | | |
| 2 | 4 | 6 | 8 | 10 | | |
| **TOTAL TEST (all multiple-choice items)** | | | | | | |

# CLASS RECORD

Teacher Name _____ Unit Skills Test _____

**Directions:** Use this chart to record results on a given Unit Skills Test for all students.

| Student | Reading: Comprehension | Reading: Word Analysis | TOTAL READING | Writing/Grammar | Writing | Study Skills | TOTAL TEST |
|---|---|---|---|---|---|---|---|
| | | | | | | | |
| | | | | | | | |
| | | | | | | | |
| | | | | | | | |
| | | | | | | | |
| | | | | | | | |
| | | | | | | | |
| | | | | | | | |
| | | | | | | | |
| | | | | | | | |
| | | | | | | | |
| | | | | | | | |
| | | | | | | | |
| | | | | | | | |
| | | | | | | | |
| | | | | | | | |
| | | | | | | | |
| | | | | | | | |
| | | | | | | | |
| | | | | | | | |
| | | | | | | | |
| | | | | | | | |
| | | | | | | | |
| | | | | | | | |
| | | | | | | | |
| | | | | | | | |
| | | | | | | | |
| | | | | | | | |

# Unit 1 Skills Test

## Focus on Family

Name _____

Date _____

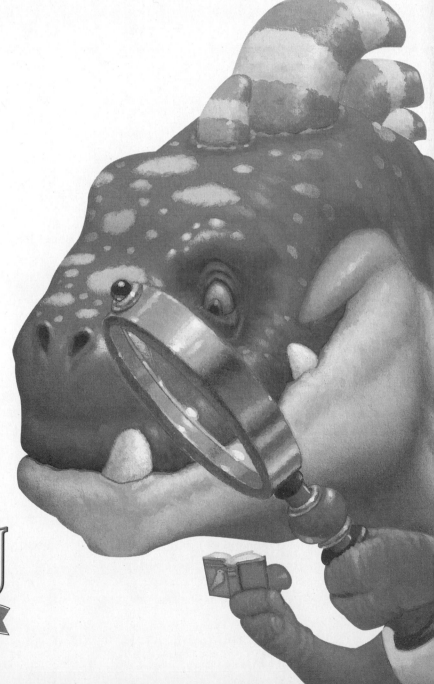

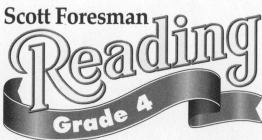

Scott Foresman
Reading
Grade 4

**Editorial Offices**
Glenview, Illinois • New York, New York

**Sales Offices**
Reading, Massachusetts • Duluth, Georgia • Glenview, Illinois
Carrollton, Texas • Menlo Park, California

ISBN 0-673-62428-5

2 3 4 5 6 7 8 9 10-EBA-06 05 04 03 02 01 00

**DIRECTIONS**

Read each passage. Then answer the questions that follow. Fill in the circle beside the best answer to each question.

# How Did Ellie Get into Trouble?

When she was a little girl, Ellie McHenry lived on a farm at the edge of a forest. Back then, life was hard. Ellie had to work all day long. She helped her mother make butter and quilts. She helped plant the corn. In the little time she had to play, she liked to pretend she was a princess or a queen. Living in a castle far away was much easier than working on the farm.

One of Ellie's jobs was to bring in the cow, Matilda, every night. Matilda roamed through the fields and into the woods during the day. At night, though, she had to be shut in the barn. There she would be safe from the wolves and wildcats.

Over and over again, Pa had told Ellie that she had to bring Matilda back before dark. Otherwise, they could both be in danger. When Ellie started daydreaming, though, she often lost track of the time.

One summer evening as the sun was setting, Pa called out to Ellie. "Time to get the cow," he said, "and don't daydream. Be sure you come right back."

Ellie was sitting by the cabin making a crown of dandelions. When she put the crown on her head, she felt like a princess. She wandered off through the fields, calling, "Here, Matilda!" The crown kept slipping down over her eyes.

GO ON

"Where are my servants?" she cried to the trees. "Where is the golden carriage to carry me back to my castle?"

Coming to the edge of a pond, she stopped to look at the water. In the reflection, she saw something move. Was it a fairy? Ellie spun around and looked up into a tree. Two bright yellow eyes gleamed down at her. It was a wildcat, ready to spring!

Suddenly, Ellie was no longer a character in a fairy tale. She did not know what to do. Should she stay still or run? Should she jump into the pond?

Then she heard a familiar noise. It was clumsy old Matilda, crashing through the forest, mooing. She sounded like a herd of cattle. The cow must have spooked the wildcat. It hissed, leaped to another tree, and disappeared into the darkness.

Ellie was so relieved that she kissed Matilda on the nose and put the crown of dandelions on her head. Then she promised Matilda that she would listen to her father's warning next time. She would not get lost in her daydreams ever again.

GO ON

1 Which sentence tells you that this story takes place in the past?
   A "The crown kept slipping down over her eyes."
   B "Back then, life was hard."
   C "One of Ellie's jobs was to bring in the cow."
   D "Otherwise, they could both be in danger."

2 How did Ellie feel when she saw the two yellow eyes?
   F amused
   G relieved
   H frightened
   J pleased

3 What kind of story is this?
   A a fairy tale
   B a mystery
   C historical fiction
   D science fiction

4 Just after Ellie saw the wildcat, she —
   F jumped into the pond.
   G looked for a fairy.
   H ran home.
   J heard Matilda.

5 In this story, the word spooked means —
   A scared off.
   B became angry.
   C gave hope to.
   D ran quickly.

6 The author's main purpose in this story is to —
   F give information.
   G describe Ellie's chores.
   H entertain readers.
   J explain how to take care of cows.

GO ON

# Paper Birds

I couldn't believe it. My teacher Mrs. Greenberg had asked for volunteers to help with our international fair. Without talking to me, my mother had asked Grandmother to visit the class. She would teach us the Asian practice of origami.

I loved my grandmother, but she was kind of embarrassing. She took tiny steps when she walked. She often wore a long kimono and special shoes that were hard to walk in. When she giggled, she held her hand to her mouth so no one would see her smile.

Her English was pretty awful besides. My name, Bruce, was simple, but she couldn't even say it. Worst of all, she bowed when she met someone she did not know.

Of course, I couldn't tell my mother how I felt. She had taught me to respect my grandparents, so I just kept my feelings to myself and worried.

When Grandmother walked into the class, she began bowing just as I had feared she would. Then Mrs. Greenberg had the whole class stand, and we all bowed in return.

Grandmother sat down and started working with colored paper. Her fingers moved quickly. She made paper birds, frogs, fish, and bugs. The kids in my class were so interested they didn't even notice that Grandmother barely spoke. Without realizing it, I started telling everyone what Grandmother was doing. I showed the other kids how to follow along with their own paper folding.

Before long, the room was filled with all kinds of paper creatures. Kids were begging for extra paper so they could make more origami.

When Grandmother was ready to leave, she started bowing again. Without a word from Mrs. Greenberg, my classmates stood. They returned her bows and then waved, calling good-by and thank you. With one hand hiding her smile, Grandmother waved back as she walked out the door.

GO ON

**7** What did Grandmother do when she first entered the classroom?

   **A** She giggled.

   **B** She waved to the students.

   **C** She bowed to the students.

   **D** She explained how to make origami.

**8** How did Bruce feel about his grandmother at the end?

   **F** proud

   **G** embarrassed

   **H** upset

   **J** sorry

**9** In this story, the word <u>origami</u> means —

   **A** a long dress worn by Asian women.

   **B** an embarrassing moment.

   **C** the practice of bowing to people.

   **D** the art of making paper figures.

**10** This story is told by —

   **F** Mrs. Greenberg.

   **G** Bruce.

   **H** Grandmother.

   **J** a third-person narrator.

**11** What is the setting of this story?

   **A** an art studio

   **B** a museum

   **C** a classroom

   **D** Bruce's home

**12** The author's main purpose in this passage is to —

   **F** entertain with a story about a boy and his grandmother.

   **G** give information about origami.

   **H** describe Grandmother.

   **J** explain how to make paper birds.

GO ON

# The Inuit Way

Many Inuit families had gathered for the winter games. They had come from all over Alaska by car, snowmobile, and airplane.

Shannon was there with her parents and her grandfather. As she walked into the huge hall, she turned to her grandfather.

"I can't wait for the blanket toss!" she exclaimed in Inuit.

"I can't wait to watch you," said Grandfather. "Too bad my old bones are too stiff to bounce on the blanket myself!"

Shannon's father smiled, the way he always did when Shannon spoke Inuit with the old people. As a child he had been sent away to an English-speaking school. When he finally came home, he couldn't speak Inuit anymore. That's why he worked so hard to make sure Shannon knew the traditional ways. She learned Inuit in school, went hunting and fishing with her uncle, and was learning how to make traditional Inuit clothes from her grandmother. Also, the family went to Inuit gatherings whenever possible, even if Shannon's father had to take time off work.

"Community is what's important," he said, "community and family. That's the Inuit way."

Inside the hall, different activities were going on. In one corner, adults and children played string games. In another corner, a man performed a skit in front of an audience.

Shannon headed for the middle of the room. About 20 Inuit stood in a circle holding a blanket that was stretched as tight as a drum. In its center stood a young man. As Shannon watched, the people catapulted the young man high into the air. A huge grin spread over his face as he flew up, nearly to the ceiling. "Whoa!" he yelled as he headed back down. He landed on the blanket and then bounced back up.

"Soon it will be your turn!" said Grandfather with a smile.

Shannon's father smiled at her too. Grandfather had spoken in Inuit, but he understood perfectly.

GO ON ▶

**13** Shannon's father believes that —
   **A** string games are fun.
   **B** family is important.
   **C** the blanket toss is silly.
   **D** the winter games go on for too long.

**14** Which of these happened first?
   **F** Shannon went hunting and fishing with her uncle.
   **G** Shannon joined the blanket toss.
   **H** Shannon learned to make traditional clothes.
   **J** Shannon's father went away to an English-speaking school.

**15** Most of this story takes place in —
   **A** a large hall.
   **B** Shannon's home.
   **C** an airplane.
   **D** a classroom.

**16** In this story, the word <u>catapulted</u> means —
   **F** yelled; shouted.
   **G** covered.
   **H** threw; tossed.
   **J** looked at.

**17** One of the author's purposes in this story is to —
   **A** give information about Inuit customs.
   **B** entertain the reader with a silly story.
   **C** persuade the reader to visit Alaska.
   **D** explain Inuit history.

**18** What kind of story is this?
   **F** science fiction
   **G** historical fiction
   **H** realistic fiction
   **J** fantasy

GO ON

# My Little Sister

Since I had always learned things faster than my little sister did, I just <u>assumed</u> she would never beat me at anything. Then Mom came home with a new computer.

"Look, Zack," said Mom after she'd finished setting it up. "It comes with all kinds of free software. It has a keyboarding program, an art program, and seven or eight games."

"Great," I answered.

I tried the keyboarding program first. I thought it would be useful to know where all the keys were without looking. But somehow, instead of flying over the keyboard, my fingers were clumsy and slow. I decided to open the art program. I thought it would be easy to draw the cool pictures in my mind, but they all came out like blobs. On to the games!

I was trying to fly a spaceship through a maze. Monsters kept jumping out and stopping me! I practiced that game for days, but I never got any better.

Then one day after school, I came into the kitchen. There was Zelda, her fingers moving over the keyboard like lightning. "Excellent," said a message on the screen. "Move on to Level 6!"

"Level 6!" I thought in amazement. I had never gotten past Level 2 in keyboarding.

That night Zelda came to dinner holding a pile of paper. "My computer drawings," she said shyly. She shouldn't have felt shy. They were really good. I started to get nervous.

Sure enough, my nightmare came true the next morning. It was a Saturday, and I asked Zelda if she had played "Maze Monsters" yet. She said no, but she'd like to try.

Within an hour she had reached the center of the Maze. I had to face it: my dopey little sister was a computer genius and I—well, I was a dope. I was feeling really angry when I noticed the expression on Zelda's face. She was glowing!

"Zack!" she said, "I'm good at something! Finally I found something I'm good at!"

"You're right," I said, although it was not easy for me to admit. "You're the greatest!"

GO ON

**19** What is the setting of this story?
- A   a library
- B   a computer store
- C   Zack's home
- D   Zelda's classroom

**20** Which sentence shows that this story is told by a first-person narrator?
- F   "It comes with all kinds of free software."
- G   "It was a Saturday, and I asked Zelda if she had played 'Maze Monsters' yet."
- H   "Within an hour she had reached the center of the Maze."
- J   "'Excellent,' said a message on the screen."

**21** In this story, the word <u>assumed</u> means —
- A   took for granted without proof; supposed.
- B   wondered about.
- C   tried hard.
- D   became successful without really trying.

**22** Just after Zack had trouble with the keyboarding program, he —
- F   played a game.
- G   taught his sister to keyboard.
- H   reached the center of the Maze.
- J   opened the art program.

**23** What did Zack realize about his sister at the end?
- A   She was upset that she had beaten him.
- B   She was proud of herself.
- C   She thought he was clumsy.
- D   She was better than him at everything.

**24** The author's main purpose in this passage is to —
- F   teach a lesson about how to use a computer.
- G   give information about mazes.
- H   describe computer games.
- J   tell how a boy learned something about his sister.

**25** What kind of story is this?
- A   fable
- B   historical fiction
- C   folk tale
- D   realistic fiction

STOP

# WRITING/GRAMMAR

**DIRECTIONS**

**Read each passage. Some parts are underlined. The underlined parts may be one of the following:**

- **Incomplete sentences**
- **Run-on sentences**
- **Correctly written sentences that should be combined**
- **Correctly written sentences that do not need to be rewritten**

**Mark the letter beside the best way to write each underlined part. If the underlined part needs no change, mark the choice "No mistake."**

---

One day I went to a store at the mall with two of my friends. I heard a

man say that we were going to have an earthquake. I quickly found my friends
                                                    (1)
told them about it.  "There's going to be an earthquake!" I yelled. They just
                                                                            (2)
laughed. They told me there has never been a big earthquake in Indiana.

Maybe the man said he was going to have a milkshake.

---

**1  A**  I quickly found my friends I told them about it.

    **B**  I quickly found my friends but told them about it.

    **C**  I quickly found my friends, and I told them about it.

    **D**  No mistake

**2  F**  They just laughed, but they

    **G**  They just laughed? They

    **H**  They just laughed, they

    **J**  No mistake

**GO ON ➤**

How would you like? To go to a dinosaur museum? Since the movie
    (3)
*Jurassic Park* came out, such museums have become very popular. At some
                                                                    (4)
museums. You can see dinosaur bones and eggs?  You can learn how

dinosaurs lived.  Also see life-size models of dinosaurs. These models show
                    (5)
scientists' views of how the dinosaurs looked.

3  A  How would you like it if you go to a dinosaur museum?
   B  How would you like to go to a dinosaur museum.
   C  How would you like to go to a dinosaur museum?
   D  No mistake

4  F  At some museums, you can see dinosaur bones and eggs.
   G  At some museums, you can see dinosaur bones and eggs?
   H  You can see dinosaur bones at some museums and eggs.
   J  No mistake

5  A  Also seeing life-size models of dinosaurs.
   B  You can also see life-size models of dinosaurs.
   C  Also, life-size models of dinosaurs can see.
   D  No mistake

STOP

# WRITING

Think about a time when someone in your family helped you do or learn something. Write a personal narrative telling about the event, who helped you, and what that person helped you do or learn.

**Prewriting Notes**

GO ON ▶

# STUDY SKILLS

**DIRECTIONS**

Imelda plans to write a report about people who lived long ago. She begins by looking for information in a textbook. Use the title page from the textbook to help answer questions 1–2.

**THE ANCIENT WORLD**

by Collin Forbes

Weston Publishing Co.
Chicago, Illinois

**1** What is the title of this book?
  **A** The Ancient World
  **B** Collin Forbes
  **C** Chicago, Illinois
  **D** Weston Publishing Co.

**2** To find the meaning of a word used in this book, Imelda should look in the —
  **F** table of contents.
  **G** glossary.
  **H** index.
  **J** captions.

GO ON

# CHAPTER 3
# ANCIENT CULTURES

## Africa

For thousands of years, the Sahara Desert separated most of Africa from the rest of the world. Beginning in about 750 A.D., many great African kingdoms rose in the lands below the Sahara. In the east was Meroë. The people of Meroë were among the earliest people to have an alphabet. They were also skilled workers in iron. In the south was Zimbabwe. This walled city was an important trading and religious center.

## The Middle East

Other great civilizations developed in what is now the Middle East. One of the greatest of these civilizations was Phoenicia. The Phoenicians were great sailors and traders. They carried cedar wood

**The Phoenicians carried on trade with swift, sleek ships.**

and a special purple cloth as far away as Spain. They developed beautiful crafts, built swift boats, and created an alphabet. Near Phoenicia, the city of Babylon became powerful about 4,000 years ago. The Babylonians created a system of laws, and they studied the movements of the stars and planets.

GO ON

**3** What is the name of this chapter?

    **A** Africa

    **B** The Middle East

    **C** Ancient Cultures

    **D** The Ancient World

**4** Which of these is a caption?

    **F** The Middle East

    **G** The Phoenicians carried on trade with swift, sleek ships.

    **H** Africa and the Middle East

    **J** Mediterranean Sea

**Use the outline below to help answer questions 5–6.**

I. Africa
   A. Meroë
   B. Zimbabwe

II. _____
   A. _____
   B. Babylon

**5** Which is the best main topic for part II of the outline?

    **A** Sahara Desert

    **B** Middle East

    **C** Great Civilizations

    **D** Babylonians

**6** Which of these should be a subtopic in part II?

    **F** Phoenicia

    **G** cedar wood

    **H** Spain

    **J** swift boats

GO ON

## DIRECTIONS

Use the table of contents and part of an index from *The Ancient World* to answer questions 7–10.

| CONTENTS | |
|---|---|
| 1. People of Long Ago | 6 |
| 2. Ancient Egypt | 24 |
| 3. Greece and Rome | 42 |
| 4. African Cultures | 60 |
| 5. Asian Cultures | 82 |
| 6. The Americas | 118 |
| Atlas | 140 |
| Glossary | 152 |

**INDEX**

**Great Rift Valley,** 61–63
**Great Wall of China,** 91
**Greece, ancient**
    city-states, 48
    farming in, 45
    geography of, 42–43
    government, 48–49
    slaves in, 47
    trade, 46

**7** In which chapter should Imelda look for information about the first peoples of North America?

  **A** Chapter 2
  **B** Chapter 3
  **C** Chapter 5
  **D** Chapter 6

**8** On which page(s) could Imelda find information about farming in ancient Greece?

  **F** pages 42–43
  **G** page 45
  **H** page 47
  **J** pages 48–49

**9** To find information about the pyramids built by rulers of ancient Egypt, Imelda should look in the index under —

  **A** builders.
  **B** ancient.
  **C** Egypt.
  **D** rulers.

**10** On what page does the chapter about African cultures begin?

  **F** page 24
  **G** page 42
  **H** page 60
  **J** page 82

STOP

## A Wider View

Name _____

Date _____

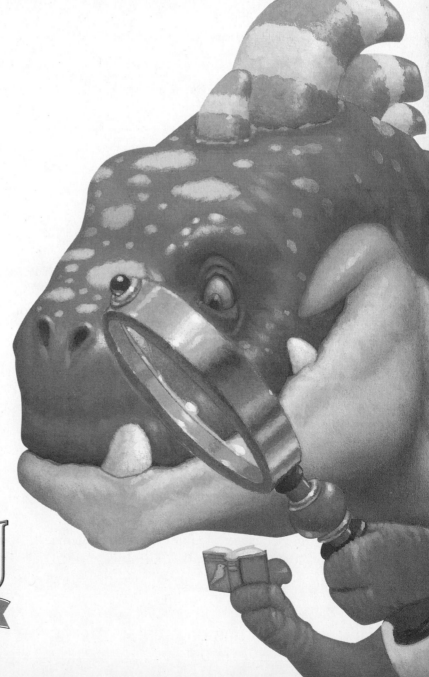

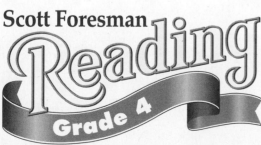

Scott Foresman
Reading
Grade 4

**Editorial Offices**
Glenview, Illinois • New York, New York

**Sales Offices**
Reading, Massachusetts • Duluth, Georgia • Glenview, Illinois
Carrollton, Texas • Menlo Park, California

ISBN 0-673-62429-3

2  3  4  5  6  7  8  9  10-EBA-06  05  04  03  02  01  00

# READING: Comprehension

**DIRECTIONS**
Read each passage. Then read the questions that follow. Choose the best answer to each question. Mark the letter for your answer.

# The Wildlife Project

"We're starting a new science project tomorrow," said Ms. Lopez to her class on Monday. "We'll be studying wildlife right here on the school playground."

That night Marna dreamed about bears and foxes. Arielle dreamed of lions. On Tuesday morning, they ran to the back of the school as soon as they got off the bus. "I guess the animals aren't here yet," said Marna. "I hope someone brings them soon."

When it was time for science, Ms. Lopez divided the class into four groups. She assigned each group a different part of the school grounds. They were to make a list of all the living creatures they saw and to notice what the creatures were doing.

When they got outside, Marna blinked in the bright sunlight. Everyone looked around eagerly, but the playground looked the same as ever. "There aren't any animals here," complained Carlos.

"Are you sure?" asked Ms. Lopez. "Listen, I hear one now."

Everyone was very quiet. At first they could only hear the rattle and roar of cars and buses on Walnut Street. Then they heard a bird chirping. A loud insect buzzed near Marna's ear. It had a long, thin body that was green and blue, and it had two sets of wings.

"There is wildlife everywhere, even in the city," said Ms. Lopez. "Look down, look up, look all around you. Make a list of the creatures you see. We will go back to the classroom in fifteen minutes to compare your lists."

Marna's group went to the part of the playground near the basketball hoop. The ground was covered with hot black asphalt. "What can we find here?" Marna said. "There's no place for animals to live."

While Marna was talking, Mario was already on his hands and knees near a crack in the asphalt. "Look at all these ants!" he said.

GO ON

Arielle peered into a clump of weeds growing next to the brick wall. She saw two insects. She didn't know their names, but she wrote down what they looked like. Then she saw some tiny ants scurrying about. "Hey look, Mario," she called, "these ants aren't black like yours. They're kind of red."

By the time they went inside, every group had at least six items on its list. The students made a chart of what they had seen.

"Next time we go out, let's make a study of just the ants," said Ms. Lopez. "Did you know that there are more than 8,000 kinds of ants in the world? I'm sure at least a few of them live here. I'd like to find out more about them."

| Wildlife Project Results | | | |
|---|---|---|---|
| Group 1 | Group 2 | Group 3 | Group 4 |
| robin | robin | blue jay | pigeon |
| blue jay | red squirrel | pigeon | gray squirrel |
| red squirrel | mouse | grasshopper | mouse |
| ants | grasshopper | beetle | cricket |
| beetle | dragonfly | ants | ants |
| earthworm | ants | bees | worms |
| | ladybugs | | slug |

GO ON

**1** Out on the playground, why did Ms. Lopez tell the class to listen?

   **A** They weren't paying attention to her.

   **B** She wanted them to notice animal sounds.

   **C** They couldn't hear the cars and trucks.

   **D** She wanted to tell them about ants.

**2** In this passage, the word <u>peered</u> means —

   **F** looked closely.

   **G** pulled apart.

   **H** wrote down.

   **J** complained loudly.

**3** Which detail helps you visualize what Marna saw on the playground?

   **A** "When they got outside, Marna blinked in the bright sunlight."

   **B** "The playground looked the same as ever."

   **C** "They could only hear the rattle and roar of cars and buses."

   **D** "It had a long, thin body that was green and blue, and it had two sets of wings."

**4** Which sentence best states the theme of this passage?

   **F** "Everyone was very quiet."

   **G** "I guess the animals aren't here yet."

   **H** "There's no place for animals to live."

   **J** "There is wildlife everywhere, even in the city."

**5** Which detail from the passage best supports the theme?

   **A** The students could hear the traffic.

   **B** Bright sunlight made the students blink.

   **C** The chart shows that every group saw at least six creatures.

   **D** There are more than 8,000 kinds of ants in the world.

**6** Which is a synonym for the word <u>divided</u> in this passage?

   **F** labeled

   **G** recorded

   **H** observed

   **J** separated

GO ON

# The Lark and the Farmer

Once there was a lark living in a cornfield with her brood of youngsters. The lark was worried about what might happen to her little ones and their home. The corn in the field was ripe, but her young ones could not yet fly. Soon the farmer would harvest the corn, and the little ones would be in danger.

As Mother Lark prepared to leave one morning to look for food, she spoke to her youngsters. "Every morning while I am gone, listen carefully. Remember anything you hear the farmer say and tell me when I return."

During the day, the little larks heard the farmer say to his son that the corn was ripe. He would ask his friends and neighbors to come and help him <u>reap</u> the corn the next day. The little ones became <u>alarmed</u>.

"Oh, we don't need to worry yet," said Mother Lark when the little ones told her what the farmer had said. "If the farmer is depending on his friends and neighbors, he will not disturb us tomorrow."

The next morning, the farmer and his son showed up early at the field. The old man waited more than an hour, but his friends and neighbors never came. "Ah, well," said the farmer, "I will call my relatives and ask them to help me tomorrow." The little larks became quite frightened.

When Mother Lark got home, the little ones again reported what the farmer had said. "We don't need to worry yet," she said. "If the farmer is depending on his relatives, he will not disturb us tomorrow."

The next morning, the farmer and his son arrived early once again. They waited for two hours, but no one else came. "Ah, well," said the farmer to his son. "We will just have to get here early tomorrow and harvest the corn ourselves."

When the little ones reported to Mother Lark that night, she was worried. "Now it's time for us to go. When a man decides to do the job himself, he will not waste any more time waiting for others."

That night Mother Lark moved her little ones to a new home away from the cornfield, and the next morning the old man and his son cut down every last stalk of corn.

GO ON

**7** Why was Mother Lark worried about when the corn would be cut down?

   **A** There would be no shade when the corn was gone.

   **B** Her little ones could not yet fly.

   **C** The farmer did not like larks.

   **D** She knew the corn was not yet ripe.

**8** Which word is a synonym for alarmed in this passage?

   **F** frightened

   **G** safe

   **H** careful

   **J** relieved

**9** What is the theme of this story?

   **A** Time you save today will be valuable tomorrow.

   **B** Farmers waste a lot of time.

   **C** Ripe corn will spoil if it is not cut right away.

   **D** If you want something done, do it yourself.

**10** Which detail best supports the theme of the story?

   **F** Mother Lark asked the little ones to listen to the farmer.

   **G** The farmer and his son got to the cornfield early.

   **H** The farmer waited for his friends and relatives, but no one showed up.

   **J** Mother Lark waited three days before moving the little ones.

**11** In this passage, the word reap means —

   **A** remember.

   **B** depend.

   **C** disturb.

   **D** harvest.

**12** What kind of selection is this?

   **F** biography

   **G** fable

   **H** tall tale

   **J** nonfiction

GO ON

# Arctic Foxes, Desert Foxes

A small fox pops out of its den by the river and trots across the flat land. The fox's grayish-blue coat blends in well with the low plants that cover the ground. The fox is heading toward the shore of the icy Arctic Ocean.

This is an arctic fox. It lives in the tundra, a treeless land with long, cold winters and short, cool summers. Cold-blooded animals, such as snakes and frogs, could never survive here, but arctic foxes are well suited for living in this harsh climate.

Arctic foxes have extremely thick fur to keep them warm. Their fur is oily to shed water. Their short ears are covered in heavy fur to keep them from losing body heat. They have fur on the bottoms of their feet to keep them from slipping on ice. The coat of the arctic fox changes color with the seasons. In winter it is white to match the snow-covered land.

The arctic fox is not the only fox that lives in a very harsh climate. Another kind of fox lives in the Sahara Desert in Africa. Some parts of the Sahara are covered with huge hills of sand as far as the eye can see. In most places, there is little to see other than bare rocks. The few plants that live there are small and far apart. The temperature is burning hot by day and freezing cold at night. The weather is so dry that some places go a year or more without rain. Most parts of the desert get a little rain each year. Few animals could survive with so little water. Yet this desert is home to some unique animals, including the fennec fox.

The fennec fox is the smallest of all foxes. Its coat is sandy colored. Its dense fur and dark eyes give it protection against the sun. During the heat of the day, the fennec fox stays under the ground. Like many desert animals, it is most <u>active</u> at night.

One thing you would notice right away if you saw a fennec fox is its huge ears. Most mammals get rid of body heat by sweating or panting. They lose water as they cool off. The fennec fox loses heat through its ears without losing water. This is one of the special ways in which the fennec fox is able to survive in one of the driest places on Earth.

GO ON ➡

13 What might you see if you were near the home of an arctic fox?

   **A** trees heavy with snow

   **B** large chunks of ice floating in the sea

   **C** tall hills of blowing sand

   **D** snakes and lizards darting under rocks

14 Which detail best helps you picture what a fennec fox looks like?

   **F** "Its coat is sandy colored."

   **G** "During the heat of the day, the fennec fox stays under the ground."

   **H** "Like many desert animals, it is most active at night."

   **J** "The fennec fox is able to survive in one of the driest places on Earth."

15 Which sentence includes sensory words?

   **A** "This is an arctic fox."

   **B** "Another kind of fox lives in the Sahara Desert."

   **C** "The temperature is burning hot by day and freezing cold at night."

   **D** "The fennec fox is the smallest of all foxes."

16 The coat of an arctic fox changes colors to help the fox —

   **F** stay warm.

   **G** lose heat without losing water.

   **H** attract other animals.

   **J** blend in with its surroundings.

17 What kind of selection is this?

   **A** expository nonfiction

   **B** folk tale

   **C** realistic fiction

   **D** fantasy

18 Which is a synonym for the word active in this passage?

   **F** sleepy

   **G** cool

   **H** lively

   **J** heavy

GO ON

# A Trip to the Museum

On Friday, all the students from Pratt Elementary School were going on a field trip to the Hope Museum. Dennis, who was in Mr. Marco's fourth-grade class, was looking forward to the trip. But he was a little worried too. On every other field trip he had ever taken, he got separated from the rest of the group like a calf cut away from the herd. When he saw something that was appealing to him, he just took off to investigate. The rest of the group was usually moving in a different direction.

On Friday morning, Dennis boarded the right bus on time and found a seat. The other kids were chattering and giggling, and sounds of their loud laughter filled the air. As soon as Dennis entered the museum, he spied some glass flowers in a room to the right. They were brightly colored, and they sparkled in the light. He just had to see them, so off he went. After a few minutes, he turned to speak to one of his friends, but no one was there. "Oh, no," he moaned, "not again." Then he remembered that Mr. Marco had given everyone in his group a schedule. Dennis pulled out the schedule to see where he was supposed to be.

| Schedule for Mr. Marco's Class | |
|---|---|
| 9:00 A.M. | Get on Bus 7. Go to museum. |
| 10:00 A.M. | Gather in museum lobby. Meet tour guide. Get list of questions. |
| 10:15 A.M. – 11:45 A.M. | Go on guided tour of dinosaur exhibit. Draw one of the dinosaurs. |
| 11:50 A.M. – 12:30 P.M. | Have lunch in museum garden. |
| 12:30 P.M. – 1:45 P.M. | Explore exhibits on floors 2 and 3. Find answers to questions on list. |
| 1:45 P.M. – 2:30 P.M. | Go to museum shop. |
| 2:30 P.M. | Get on Bus 7. Return to school. |

19  Dennis was worried about the field trip because he —
    A   did not have any money.
    B   always got lost on field trips.
    C   could not answer the questions on the list.
    D   did not like museums.

20  In this passage, the word appealing means —
    F   interesting.
    G   closed.
    H   pretty.
    J   strange.

21  Which sentence from the passage uses imagery?
    A   "On Friday, all the students from Pratt Elementary School were going on a field trip to the Hope Museum."
    B   "On Friday morning, Dennis boarded the right bus on time."
    C   "The other kids were chattering and giggling, and sounds of their loud laughter filled the air."
    D   "The rest of the group was usually moving in a different direction."

22  Which is a synonym for the word spied in this passage?
    F   worried
    G   investigated
    H   walked
    J   noticed

23  Which sentence helps you picture what Dennis saw in the museum?
    A   "They were brightly colored, and they sparkled in the light."
    B   "After a few minutes, he turned to speak to one of his friends."
    C   "He just took off to investigate."
    D   "He just had to see them, so off he went."

24  In this passage, what are exhibits?
    F   lists of events and times
    G   things that are shown in public
    H   school buses
    J   items for sale in a store

STOP

# WRITING/GRAMMAR

## DIRECTIONS

**Read the passage. Choose the word or group of words that belongs in each numbered blank. Mark the letter for your answer.**

---

Carla walked slowly down _____. She was on her way to the dentist to
                          (1)

have her _____ cleaned. Trudy, the _____ assistant, spent more than an
         (2)                      (3)

hour with Carla. Then _____ came in to see her. Unfortunately, he found
                      (4)

three _____, so Carla will have to go back again next week. Trudy gave
      (5)

her some _____ toothbrushes and floss to take home.
         (6)

---

1 A  third street

   B  Third Street

   C  third Street

   D  Third street


2 F  tooths

   G  toothes

   H  teeth

   J  teeths


3 A  dentist's

   B  dentist

   C  dentists

   D  dentists'


4 F  dr. moore

   G  Dr. moore

   H  dr. Moore

   J  Dr. Moore


5 A  cavity

   B  cavities

   C  cavitys

   D  cavityes


6 F  children's

   G  children

   H  childrens

   J  childrens'

# WRITING

Write a description of where you live. You might want to describe your house or apartment, or you might describe your room. Help readers use their senses to picture where you live.

**Prewriting Notes**

GO ON ➡

# STUDY SKILLS

## DIRECTIONS

Steve is looking for information about animals for a report. Use the pictures of a newspaper and three magazines to answer questions 1–3. Mark the letter for your answer.

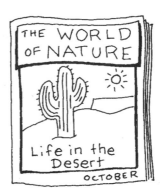

GO ON ▶

1 Steve wants to find information about a gorilla that was born yesterday in the San Diego Zoo. In which periodical should he look?

   **A** *San Diego News*

   **B** *Seven Days*

   **C** *The World of Nature*

   **D** *Animals Magazine*

2 Which periodical is most likely to have an article about giraffes?

   **F** *San Diego News*

   **G** *Seven Days*

   **H** *The World of Nature*

   **J** *Animals Magazine*

3 Which of these articles would most likely be found in *Seven Days* magazine?

   **A** "Vacationing Along the Coral Reefs"

   **B** "New President Elected in Brazil"

   **C** "Mayor Clark to Speak at Luncheon Today"

   **D** "How Toads Survive in the Desert"

GO ON

**Steve found this chart about different kinds of animals. Use the chart to answer questions 4–7.**

| Group | Characteristics | Examples |
|-------|----------------|----------|
| Mammals | Warm-blooded<br>Covered with hair or fur<br>Babies are born live and are fed by mother. | cats and dogs<br>monkeys<br>cows |
| Reptiles | Cold-blooded<br>Covered with dry scales or horny plates<br>Babies are hatched from eggs and take care of themselves from birth. | snakes<br>turtles<br>alligators |
| Amphibians | Cold-blooded<br>Most have smooth, moist skin.<br>Live in water and on land<br>Babies are born from eggs in water and go through tadpole stage. | frogs<br>salamanders |
| Marsupials | Warm-blooded mammals<br>Babies live in a pouch on the mother's body. | kangaroos<br>opossums |

GO ON

**4** The first column of the chart lists —

  **F** groups of animals.

  **G** what animals look like.

  **H** examples of mammals.

  **J** where animals live.

**5** How are reptiles different from mammals?

  **A** Reptiles are warm-blooded.

  **B** Reptiles' skin is covered with scales.

  **C** Reptiles are born live.

  **D** Reptiles go through a tadpole stage.

**6** Which of these is an amphibian?

  **F** monkey

  **G** kangaroo

  **H** alligator

  **J** salamander

**7** What is unusual about marsupials?

  **A** Babies are hatched from eggs.

  **B** They have smooth skin.

  **C** Babies live in the mother's pouch.

  **D** They are warm-blooded.

GO ON

**Steve found this encyclopedia entry about newts. Use the entry to help answer questions 8–10.**

> **newt,** a member of the SALAMANDER family. Newts are shaped like lizards and are 2-6 inches long (5-15 cm). Many newts are brightly colored, such as the red-spotted newt. Most newts are born in water, where they breathe through gills. Later they develop lungs, move to the land, and are called efts. Adults return to the water to lay eggs.

8 Which of these entries would appear before **newt** in the encyclopedia?
   F   nighthawk
   G   narwhal
   H   nuthatch
   J   node

9 In which volume of the encyclopedia would this entry appear?
   A   Vol. 9: M-N
   B   Vol. 10: O-P
   C   Vol. 11: Q-R
   D   Vol. 12: S

10 If Steve wanted to find more information about newts, he should look in the encyclopedia under what other key word?
   F   family
   G   lizard
   H   salamander
   J   member

STOP

# Unit 3 Skills Test

## Keys to Success

Name _____

Date _____

**Scott Foresman**
Reading
Grade 4

**Editorial Offices**
Glenview, Illinois • New York, New York

**Sales Offices**
Reading, Massachusetts • Duluth, Georgia • Glenview, Illinois
Carrollton, Texas • Menlo Park, California

ISBN 0-673-62430-7

2 3 4 5 6 7 8 9 10-EBA-06 05 04 03 02 01 00

**DIRECTIONS**

Read each passage. Then read the questions that follow. Choose the best answer to each question. Mark the letter for your answer.

# Why I Became a Vet

I love animals. I've always loved animals. That's probably the reason I became a veterinarian.

When I was a little girl, I lived in an apartment over my parents' store. My mother and father were busy from morning until night, six days a week. They weren't interested in having pets around the house.

Luckily for me, my cousin Tom lived on a ranch just a few miles away. I spent as much time as possible out at the ranch. That's where I learned to ride and groom horses. It's where I first watched a cat take care of her newborn kittens. It's also where I learned what a special friend a dog can be.

Tom's family had three dogs. Hector and Lucy were working dogs. They stayed outdoors or in the stables most of the time. Paco was Tom's pet. He slept in the house and followed us wherever we went. Sometimes I thought of him as my dog too.

One hot day when I was nine years old, Tom and I were playing pirates down by the river. The river was high and the current was very fast. I knew I was not supposed to go in the water, but I wanted to cool off. I was a strong

GO ON ➡

swimmer and felt very sure of myself, so I stepped down the steep bank and into the water. I lost my balance almost immediately. The swift current grabbed at my legs and swept me away.

Tom ran along the bank calling my name, but he couldn't keep up. Paco <u>heard</u> his cries and raced to a bend in the river. As the river swept me around the bend, Paco leaped in and dragged me to safety. It was the scariest moment of my life and one I will never forget.

Maybe that was the day when I first knew I would spend my life taking care of animals. From that time on, I put extra effort into my science courses in school. All veterinarians love science, but I knew I would have to work very hard to get into college and become a vet.

My hard work paid off. Although Paco, the hero of my childhood, is long gone now, it gives me great pleasure to help other dogs live happy, healthy lives. For me, being a vet is the best job in the world.

GO ON

1 Which word best describes the narrator's behavior when she decided to go into the river?

A brave
B sensible
C lazy
D foolish

2 In this passage, the word <u>heard</u> means —

F a group of animals of one kind.
G guide or drive a group in a particular direction.
H took in sounds through the ear.
J a large number of people.

3 How did the narrator feel about school?

A She was determined to succeed.
B School was easy and fun.
C She didn't like studying.
D School seemed like a waste of time.

4 Which sentence from the passage is a generalization?

F "Sometimes I thought of him as my dog too."
G "All veterinarians love science."
H "It gives me great pleasure to help other dogs."
J "Paco leaped in and dragged me to safety."

5 For the vet in this passage, what is the most important thing about her job?

A It is hard work.
B She can help animals.
C It pays well.
D She can have her own dog.

6 What kind of selection is this?

F fantasy
G tall tale
H mystery
J autobiography

GO ON

# Pecos Bill

Pecos Bill was by all accounts the most remarkable cowboy that ever lived. He was raised by a pack of coyotes and never did learn any manners. He defeated all the bad men in Texas, and then he headed west. He was looking to join up with the meanest, roughest bunch of cowboys he could find. He had heard tell of such an outfit about two hundred miles away. He set out to find them.

A hundred miles down a steep canyon, Pecos Bill's horse broke a leg. So Bill slung the saddle over his shoulder and set off on foot. He hadn't gone far when a ten-foot rattlesnake challenged him to a fight. Bill put down his saddle. He gave the snake the first three bites, just to be fair. Then he lit into that reptile and knocked the poison right out of him. Soon Bill was on his way again, the saddle in one hand and the snake in the other.

After about fifty miles, he heard a mighty roar. A giant mountain lion leaped down onto Bill's back. Chuckling to himself, Bill put down the saddle and the snake. Soon fur was flying. Before long the lion was hollering, "I give up! Can't you take a joke?"

Bill stopped fighting and cinched his saddle on the lion. He rode on, whooping and hollering and swinging the rattlesnake. That lion was going a hundred feet at a jump! It wasn't long before they came upon a bunch of cowboys around a fire. Bill rode up and climbed off the lion's back.

Being hungry, and seeing a pot of beans on the fire, Bill scooped out a few handfuls and swallowed them. He washed them down with a few pots of boiling coffee. Then he wiped his mouth with a cactus and asked, "Who's the boss of this outfit?"

A large man about eight feet tall stood up and said, "I used to be, Stranger, but you are now."

GO ON

**7** Pecos Bill was best known for his —

   **A** strength.

   **B** cleverness.

   **C** kindness.

   **D** good manners.

**8** How did Bill feel when the mountain lion attacked him?

   **F** frightened

   **G** annoyed

   **H** amused

   **J** worn out

**9** Based on this passage, which is a valid generalization?

   **A** No creature dared to challenge Pecos Bill.

   **B** Pecos Bill liked all animals.

   **C** Everyone liked Pecos Bill.

   **D** No one could beat Pecos Bill.

**10** From his words to Pecos Bill, what can you tell about the boss of the cowboys?

   **F** He knew Bill was tougher than he.

   **G** He wanted to get rid of Bill.

   **H** He was looking for a fight.

   **J** He wanted to impress Bill.

**11** Why did the mountain lion say, "Can't you take a joke?"

   **A** He wanted to pick a fight.

   **B** He wanted Bill to believe that he had never meant to harm him.

   **C** When he first jumped on Bill, he was trying to be funny.

   **D** He thought Bill needed to change his ways.

**12** What kind of selection is this?

   **F** autobiography

   **G** biography

   **H** realistic fiction

   **J** tall tale

GO ON

# Taking Care of a Horse

A hundred years ago, many families owned horses. In those days, horses and ponies did lots of useful work. They were especially important for getting people where they wanted to go. Families needed horses, much as they need cars today.

Now that we don't depend on horses anymore, fewer families have them. Still, everyone wants a horse. You may have dreamed of owning one yourself. In your dreams you may be galloping as fast as the wind down a quiet country road or brushing your horse's glossy coat for a big horse show.

If you own a horse or pony, you already know that dreaming about a horse is easier than owning one. You need to take care of your horse every day, both before and after school.

The chart below will give you an idea of what a normal daily routine might be for a horse owner, whether you keep your horse at home or board it at a stable.

Would you like doing all these things for your horse each day? Horses need a lot of attention, and they also cost a lot of money. You'll need to pay for feed, supplies, and bills from your vet. That is why, for many horse lovers, owning a horse remains only a dream.

### Morning

| |
|---|
| 1.  Check the horse. Clean its feet. |
| 2.  Turn it out into the field. Let it stay out as long as possible. Make sure there is plenty of water for it to drink. |
| 3.  Clean out the stall. Let the floor dry before putting down clean bedding. |
| 4.  Fill the hay net or hay rack. |

### Afternoon or Evening

| |
|---|
| 1.  Catch the horse if it is in the field. |
| 2.  Clean its feet and give it a light grooming. |
| 3.  Ride or exercise the horse. |
| 4.  If it is sweaty, give it a sponge bath. In cold weather, dry the horse and put on a stable blanket. |
| 5.  Feed the horse. |

**13** Which sentence states a generalization?

  **A** "Turn it out into the field."

  **B** "You may have dreamed of owning one yourself."

  **C** "Everyone wants a horse."

  **D** "You'll need to pay for feed."

**14** More families owned horses a hundred years ago because back then —

  **F** horses did not require as much care.

  **G** more people liked horses.

  **H** people used horses for transportation.

  **J** fewer children went to school.

**15** If you owned a horse, what would be the most important thing you would need to do before going on vacation?

  **A** have someone check on the horse once a week

  **B** put the horse outside

  **C** sell the horse or give it away

  **D** have someone care for the horse twice each day

**16** Who could best use the information in this passage?

  **F** someone who wants to know what owning a horse involves

  **G** someone who is trying to choose a pet

  **H** someone who owns a horse

  **J** someone who wants to learn to ride a horse

**17** Which sentence from the passage includes a simile?

  **A** "Families needed horses."

  **B** "In your dreams you may be galloping as fast as the wind."

  **C** "Let it stay out as long as possible."

  **D** "Would you like doing all these things for your horse each day?"

**18** In this passage, the word <u>board</u> means —

  **F** a piece of wood.

  **G** to cover with wood.

  **H** tired of; uninterested.

  **J** to pay for room and food.

GO ON

# Tryouts for the School Play

**Calling all actors!**

It's the moment you've been waiting for! It's time for the spring play!

Come to Ms. Kroll's classroom on Tuesday, March 3, at 3:30 to find out about this year's play. Maybe there's a part for you!

If you want to be in the cast, you must sign up for a tryout on the schedule in the <u>main</u> office. Tryouts will be held on Wednesday, Thursday, and Friday.

**Calling musicians too!**

This year's play needs a band! If you play an instrument and want to be in the show, talk with Mr. Woods.

**Would you rather work behind the <u>scene</u>?**

Maybe you're a shrinking violet. Don't let that stop you. There's a lot more to putting on a play than being out on stage. Can you draw or sew? Do you like to write? Do you have a flair for building things? There's definitely a place for you on the crew.

Anyone interested in working on sets, costumes, or publicity should sign up with Ms. Kroll. She is also looking for students to help backstage.

**This year's play needs a large cast and crew! Surely there's something that you could do! Don't be shy! Give it a try!**

**Come to the information meeting on March 3.**

GO ON

**19** What conclusion can you draw about Mr. Woods?

    **A** He will choose the musicians for the show.

    **B** He teaches fourth grade.

    **C** He will be the director for the show.

    **D** He is the school principal.

**20** Students who can sew would be best suited for what jobs?

    **F** crew members

    **G** actors

    **H** band members

    **J** writers

**21** In this announcement, the word scene means —

    **A** observed or watched.

    **B** the stage set for a play.

    **C** show of strong feeling.

    **D** to write one's name.

**22** In this announcement, the word main means —

    **F** one of the northeastern states.

    **G** a large pipe.

    **H** the hair on a horse's neck and head.

    **J** most important.

**23** Which sentence from the announcement includes a metaphor?

    **A** "It's time for the spring play!"

    **B** "Maybe there's a part for you!"

    **C** "Maybe you're a shrinking violet."

    **D** "Do you have a flair for building things?"

**24** What generalization can you make based on the announcement?

    **F** All students are welcome to try out for the school play.

    **G** Everyone wants to be an actor.

    **H** Students who can draw or build are more important than actors.

    **J** Everyone who plays an instrument will be in the band.

**STOP**

# READING: Word Analysis

**DIRECTIONS**
Choose the correct form of the word to complete each sentence.

25 Our class has two _____.
   A  teacher's
   B  teacher
   C  teacheres
   D  teachers

26 Anita planted four _____ of beans.
   F  row
   G  rowes
   H  rows
   J  row's

27 Mom poured three _____ of milk.
   A  glasses
   B  glass
   C  glassies
   D  glases

28 Dan fed the two _____.
   F  pony
   G  ponys
   H  ponyes
   J  ponies

29 Jenny made three _____.
   A  wishs
   B  wish
   C  wishes
   D  wishies

30 Her birthday was six _____ ago.
   F  monthes
   G  month's
   H  month
   J  months

STOP

# WRITING/GRAMMAR

## DIRECTIONS
Read each passage. Choose the word or words that best fit in each numbered blank. Mark the letter for your answer.

---

I have two best friends, Jaime and Allen. I _____ baseball, but Allen
                                            **(1)**

and Jamie do not. We all play basketball, though. Allen comes over to my

house every day, and he always _____ a basketball.
                               **(2)**

---

1 A likes
  B like
  C liking
  D will like

2 F bring
  G brought
  H was bringing
  J brings

GO ON

Every year, dozens of tornadoes strike Kansas. When I was a little

girl, a tornado _____ through my hometown. Many houses were
      (3)
destroyed. Many people _____ all their belongings. Now my family is
                (4)
packing to leave. We _____ to Minnesota next week. I hope there are no
            (5)
tornadoes there!

3  A  will come
   B  comes
   C  came
   D  coming

4  F  lose
   G  will lose
   H  are losing
   J  lost

5  A  will move
   B  moves
   C  were moving
   D  moved

STOP

# WRITING

Think about two places you have lived or two places you have visited. Write a comparison/contrast essay telling how the two places are alike and how they are different.

**Prewriting Notes**

GO ON

STOP

# STUDY SKILLS

**DIRECTIONS**

Tina is looking for books about building boats. When she searches the library database, this screen appears. Use the screen to help answer the questions.

| Subject/Titles | Call Number |
|---|---|
| **Boats** | |
| 1) Boats, Trains, and Planes | 388 |
| 2) How to Build a Sailboat | 623.822 |
| 3) Jason, the Boat Builder | CAL |
| 4) Sailing to Maine | 917.41 |

Type a number to find out more about a title. ☐

Type A, T, or S to begin a new search. ☐

**1** This screen shows the results of a search by —
A author.
B title.
C subject.
D call number.

**2** Which book on the list is fiction?
F *Boats, Trains, and Planes*
G *Sailing to Maine*
H *How to Build a Sailboat*
J *Jason, the Boat Builder*

**3** What is the call number for *How to Build a Sailboat?*
A 388
B 623.822
C CAL
D 917.41

GO ON

**DIRECTIONS**

**Tina plays softball for the Blackstone Barracudas. Use the schedule below to answer the questions.**

**Softball Schedule: Blackstone Barracudas**

| Date | Team | Location | Time |
|------|------|----------|------|
| Apr. 5 | Whitefish | home | 3:45 |
| Apr. 11 | Striders | Whitegate | 5:00 |
| Apr. 15 | Tornadoes | Emerson | 5:00 |
| Apr. 22 | Striders | home | 5:00 |
| Apr. 29 | Cougars | home | 3:45 |
| May 3 | Whitefish | Sunnyside | 3:45 |
| May 10 | Cougars | Holly Hill | 5:00 |
| May 19 | Tornadoes | home | 3:45 |

**4** Which team will the Barracudas play on April 15?

   **F** Tornadoes

   **G** Whitefish

   **H** Cougars

   **J** Striders

**5** On May 3, the Barracudas will play at —

   **A** Whitegate.

   **B** Sunnyside.

   **C** Emerson.

   **D** home.

STOP

# Unit 4 Skills Test

## Timeless Stories

Name _____

Date _____

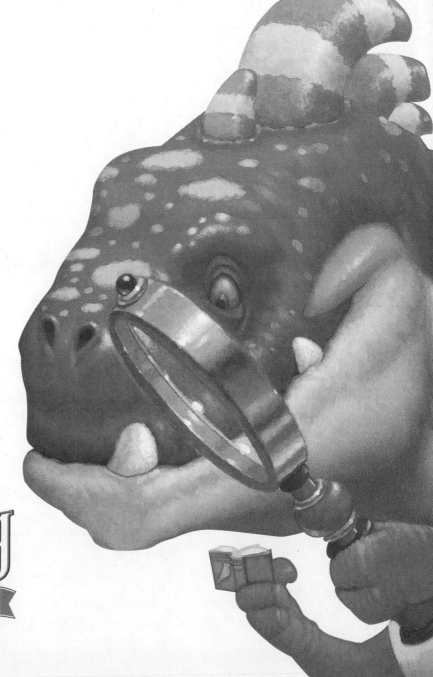

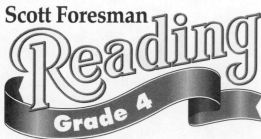

Scott Foresman
Reading
Grade 4

**Editorial Offices**
Glenview, Illinois • New York, New York

**Sales Offices**
Reading, Massachusetts • Duluth, Georgia • Glenview, Illinois
Carrollton, Texas • Menlo Park, California

ISBN 0-673-62431-5

2 3 4 5 6 7 8 9 10-EBA-06 05 04 03 02 01 00

# READING: Comprehension

**DIRECTIONS**
Read each passage. Then read the questions that follow. Choose the best answer to each question. Mark the letter for your answer.

# Rabbit and Tiger

Long ago, all the creatures of the jungle got along just fine, except one. Tiger wanted to eat everyone else, so it's not surprising that the other animals distrusted him. Tiger especially wanted to eat Rabbit, but Rabbit was quick and clever, and he delighted in playing tricks on Tiger.

One hot sultry day, Rabbit was making a rope out of some vines when Tiger came sneaking up behind him.

"I've caught you now!" said Tiger triumphantly. "You're one dead rabbit."

Rabbit had to think fast. "Okay, Tiger," he said. "Just eat me up right now, quickly, so I won't have to be around when the hurricane hits."

"The hurricane?" said Tiger. "You know how I hate hurricanes!"

"I hate them too," said Rabbit. "That's why I'm making this rope. I'm going to tie myself down to something so I don't blow away."

"That's an <u>excellent</u> idea," said Tiger. "Tie me down too. I don't want to blow away either."

So Rabbit tied Tiger to a sturdy tree. He wrapped lengths of his rope around and around Tiger, and then he pulled it very tight. Before Tiger could utter another word, Rabbit was gone!

GO ON ➡

Now, as you know, Tiger was by no means the most popular guy in the jungle. It took him two whole days to talk anyone into helping him. At last, a couple of monkeys agreed to help. As they untied him, Tiger grabbed one of the monkeys and started to pop her into his mouth, but just then he heard a voice from up in the tree.

"Foolish Tiger, don't you know how to eat a monkey?"

"Well, I thought I did," said Tiger.

"To do it properly, you've got to throw the monkey up into the air," said the voice. "Then close your eyes, open your mouth, and let the monkey fall in."

Tiger shrugged. "Okay," he said, and he repeated the instructions to himself as he tossed the monkey into the air. The monkey caught hold of a branch and scampered away.

Rabbit, who was up in the tree, tossed a seedpod into Tiger's open mouth. Tiger coughed and sputtered until the seedpod flew out. Then he ran off through the jungle roaring, "I'll get you for this! You're one dead rabbit."

Rabbit just sat up in that tree and had a good long laugh.

GO ON ▶

1 What is Tiger's main problem in this story?

  **A** The other animals cannot get along.

  **B** Tiger feels lonely without any friends.

  **C** Tiger cannot find enough food to eat.

  **D** Rabbit keeps playing tricks on him.

2 Compared with Tiger, Rabbit is —

  **F** stronger.

  **G** less popular.

  **H** smarter.

  **J** more honest.

3 Based on previous meetings, what will most likely happen the next time Rabbit and Tiger meet?

  **A** Rabbit will trick Tiger.

  **B** Rabbit and Tiger will become friends.

  **C** Tiger will eat Rabbit.

  **D** Rabbit will help other monkeys.

4 What kind of selection is this?

  **F** mystery

  **G** realistic fiction

  **H** historical fiction

  **J** folk tale

5 Which word means the opposite of the word <u>excellent</u> in this story?

  **A** terrific

  **B** thoughtful

  **C** terrible

  **D** funny

6 The story says, "Now, as you know, Tiger was by no means the most popular guy in the jungle." Which is the best paraphrase of this sentence?

  **F** Tiger was no longer as popular as he used to be, as you know.

  **G** Tiger was not well liked in the jungle.

  **H** Tiger was well liked, except in the jungle.

  **J** Tiger was the second most popular guy in the jungle.

GO ON

# The Art of Storytelling

Everybody loves a good story. Stories tell us what life is all about. Some stories are a lot more entertaining than others, of course. Some storytellers are a lot better than others too! You might hang on every word as someone relates a story about a trip to the local supermarket because you don't want to miss any details. Yet another person bores you stiff while telling about an adventure on the Amazon River. It's all in how the story is told.

## History of Storytelling

Long ago, there were storytellers who had the job of memorizing many stories. They told their stories again and again and then passed them on to younger storytellers. In this way, stories lived on for hundreds of years without ever being written down.

To remember the stories, storytellers often told them as poems or songs. Sometimes they added sound effects. Sometimes they used dances or masks to help tell a story.

After writing was invented, no one needed to memorize the stories anymore. However, people did not want to stop listening to stories told aloud just because they could read them.

## Today's Storytellers

Today's stories are often told by people who act them out in a stage play, movie, or TV show. Different actors play the parts of different characters. Costumes, make-up, and painted sets are often used to show the audience how the people and places look.

Old-fashioned storytellers are still around too. They do not need costumes, sets, or other actors. They paint the story's scenes with their words and use different voices or ways of speaking to bring the characters to life.

If you want to become a storyteller, you will have to work at it. No matter how you choose to present your story, you will need to plan it and rehearse it. Before you do that, you must take care of the most important step of all: finding the story you want to tell.

GO ON

**7** You can predict that the next section of this article will be about how to —

   **A** put on a stage play.

   **B** make a movie or TV show.

   **C** find a story to tell.

   **D** rehearse a performance.

**8** How are old-fashioned storytelling and stage plays alike?

   **F** Costumes and make-up help you know what the characters look like.

   **G** Different actors play different characters.

   **H** There are usually painted sets.

   **J** The story is performed for an audience.

**9** Which phrase from the story is an idiom?

   **A** "needed to memorize the stories"

   **B** "hang on every word"

   **C** "used dances or masks"

   **D** "how the people and places look"

**10** What is the opposite of the word <u>entertaining</u> in this article?

   **F** boring

   **G** humorous

   **H** educational

   **J** exciting

**11** What is the opposite of the word <u>often</u>?

   **A** seldom

   **B** nicely

   **C** well

   **D** simply

**12** The story says, "People did not want to stop listening to stories told aloud just because they could read them." Which is the best paraphrase of this sentence?

   **F** People started reading stories aloud.

   **G** Because they were reading stories, people could not hear them.

   **H** People still wanted to hear stories even though they could read them.

   **J** Because they could read stories, people did not want to hear them anymore.

GO ON

# Stealing the Smell:
## A Story from Peru

There once was a baker
    who worked hard all day.
He was much too stingy
    to give food away.
Not a crumb would he give
    to a bird or a beast,
Though he had enough bread
    to put on a feast.

Next door lived a poor man
    who greeted each day
By enjoying the fine smells
    that came his way.
The baker was angry.
    "That lazy oaf —
He steals the fragrance
    while I bake the loaf!"

He said to his neighbor,
    "Now listen to me,
From now on you'll not have
    these fine smells for free.
Ten gold coins each month
    is what you must pay,
Or I'll take you to court
    to get my own way."

"You're pulling my leg,"
    the neighbor said.
He did not pay coins
    but smiled kindly instead.

The baker then sued,
    and the judge agreed
To try the case
    with all due speed.

He ordered the neighbor
    to come for a hearing
And bring ten gold coins.
    (The baker was cheering!)
"Is it true," asked the judge,
    "what the baker is saying?
You've enjoyed his smells
    without ever paying?"

The neighbor agreed,
    indeed it was true.
The judge said, "Then this is
    what you must do.
Take out your purse
    and shake the coins around."
Then he asked the baker,
    "Do you like the sound?"

"Oh, yes," said the baker
    with a very big grin,
As he thought of the riches
    he thought he would win.
"Then this case is settled.
    It has ended well.
You've been paid with a sound
    for the use of a smell."

GO ON ➡

13 What is the main conflict in this poem?

   A   A neighbor is stealing from the baker.
   B   The baker wants his neighbor to pay for the smells he enjoys.
   C   The judge wants to settle the case quickly.
   D   The baker has too much bread.

14 The conflict is resolved when the —

   F   baker tells his neighbor to pay.
   G   neighbor gives the baker a smile.
   H   judge lets the sound of the coins be payment to the baker.
   J   baker grins at the sound of the coins.

15 After the case is settled, the neighbor most likely will —

   A   give his coins to the baker.
   B   continue smelling the bread.
   C   ask the baker for a job.
   D   become a baker himself.

16 Compared with his neighbor, the baker is —

   F   poorer.
   G   more clever.
   H   lazier.
   J   more selfish.

17 Which is an example of an idiom?

   A   "You're pulling my leg"
   B   "Next door lived a poor man"
   C   "Ten gold coins each month"
   D   "He did not pay coins"

18 The poem says, "The judge agreed to try the case with all due speed." Which is the best paraphrase of this sentence?

   F   The judge agreed that the case wouldn't require much speed.
   G   The judge agreed to hold the trial very soon.
   H   The judge agreed to make speed an issue in the case.
   J   The judge agreed that the case was due to speed.

GO ON

# PLAYBILL

## Sara Sleuth and the Case of the Stolen Art

A Mystery in One Act
by Mackenzie Foster

### The Characters

**Sara Sleuth,** a ten-year-old amateur detective, is visiting her elderly aunt.

**Aunt Cecily** lives in an old house in San Francisco.

**Officer Wright,** a police detective, is Aunt Cecily's son.

**Mr. Doolittle** is Aunt Cecily's new neighbor.

**Emilio Lopez** is a scientist visiting Aunt Cecily.

**Sonia DeFeliciano** is a movie producer from Hollywood.

**Mrs. Arnold** is Aunt Cecily's new housekeeper.

**Scene 1:** Aunt Cecily's living room, just before dinner
**Scene 2:** Outside Aunt Cecily's house
**Scene 3:** Aunt Cecily's dining room
**Scene 4:** Aunt Cecily's dining room, later that night

### The Cast

| | |
|---|---|
| Sara | Tonia Graham |
| Aunt Cecily | Lani Sanchez |
| Officer Wright | Joey Detroit |
| Mr. Doolittle | Alex Ciardi |
| Emilio Lopez | Tony Zuar |
| Sonia DeFeliciano | Nadia Fine |
| Mrs. Arnold | Christine Baker |

### The Production Staff

| | |
|---|---|
| Director | Maria Oliveira |
| Stage Manager | Dan Freeman |
| Costumes | Sally Diamond |
| Set Design | Mackenzie Foster |

### About the Playwright

Mackenzie Foster is a senior at Baileyville High School. She got the idea for writing this play from an actual crime that took place in California a few years ago. A valuable work of art was stolen from the home of an elderly woman. A young girl found the clues that led to the thief. This is Miss Foster's first play.

Refreshments will be sold in the lobby. The audience is asked to refrain from bringing any food or drink into the auditorium.

19 "Sara Sleuth and the Case of the Stolen Art" is a —
A drama.
B narrative poem.
C novel.
D folk tale.

20 You can tell that the central problem in the plot is that —
F Mr. Lopez has discovered a science mystery.
G the dinner party is interrupted by a strange noise outdoors.
H someone has stolen a work of art.
J a Hollywood producer has a strange interest in Aunt Cecily's house.

21 Which character will most likely solve the mystery?
A Aunt Cecily
B Officer Wright
C Emilio Lopez
D Sara Sleuth

22 Sara is different from all of the other characters because she is —
F a guest.
G a child.
H Aunt Cecily's relative.
J a detective.

23 The opposite of the word elderly is —
A lively.
B grand.
C young.
D poor.

24 On the playbill is the sentence, "The audience is asked to refrain from bringing any food or drink into the auditorium." Which is the best paraphrase of this sentence?
F Please do not eat or drink in the auditorium.
G Leave the audience's food and drink in the auditorium.
H Please use the auditorium for eating and drinking.
J Eating and drinking will take place during the play.

STOP

# READING: Word Analysis

**DIRECTIONS**
Choose the correct form of the word to complete each sentence. Mark the letter for your answer.

25  Sherry _____ to the bus every morning.
   A  rush
   B  rushs
   C  rush's
   D  rushes

26  On Saturdays, Jed _____ bikes in his garage.
   F  fix
   G  fixes
   H  fixs
   J  fix's

27  Charlene _____ her friend Jan.
   A  misses
   B  miss
   C  miss's
   D  mises

**DIRECTIONS**
Read the underlined word. Find the part of the word that is a suffix. Mark the letter for your answer.

28  careful
   F  care
   G  are
   H  ref
   J  ful

29  excitement
   A  ment
   B  cite
   C  ent
   D  excite

30  happiness
   F  happy
   G  ness
   H  pin
   J  ess

STOP

# WRITING/GRAMMAR

## DIRECTIONS

**Read each passage. Choose the word or words that best fit in each numbered blank. Mark the letter for your answer.**

---

Uncle George has two skinny hogs and an old, _____ horse on his farm.
**(1)**

Uncle George is not much of a farmer, but I really enjoy visiting him. His

farm is the _____ place I have ever been.
**(2)**

---

1 **A** buy
**B** kindness
**C** tired
**D** lazily

2 **F** most peacefulest
**G** most peaceful
**H** peacefuler
**J** peaceful

GO ON ➡

Henry stood at the corner and waited _____ for the traffic light to
                                              (3)
change. It was _____ than he thought, so he rushed into the street. A car
                    (4)
honked at him, and he jumped back on the curb. He would be _____
                                                               (5)
next time.

3  **A**  anxiously
   **B**  noise
   **C**  nervous
   **D**  excite

4  **F**  later
   **G**  lately
   **H**  latest
   **J**  late

5  **A**  carefuller
   **B**  carefullest
   **C**  more careful
   **D**  most careful

STOP

# WRITING

Are you good at washing a car or planning a party? Can you make an egg salad sandwich? Think of something you know how to do well.

Write a how-to report telling how to do the task you choose. Be sure to explain all the steps in the process.

**Prewriting Notes**

GO ON

# STUDY SKILLS

**DIRECTIONS**

**Cal is looking for reference sources to help in writing a report about the history of baseball. Look at the tables of contents from two books he has found. Choose the best answer to each question.**

| Baseball Greats | |
|---|---|
| **Chapter** | **Page** |
| 1  Babe Ruth | 1 |
| 2  Ty Cobb | 21 |
| 3  Lou Gehrig | 37 |
| 4  Satchel Paige | 51 |
| 5  The Hall of Fame | 67 |

| The History of Baseball | |
|---|---|
| **Chapter** | **Page** |
| 1  How Baseball Began | 3 |
| 2  Early Heroes | 17 |
| 3  The Major Leagues | 31 |
| 4  Today's Players | 45 |

1  *The History of Baseball* would be the better source of information about —

   **A**  Ty Cobb's years as a player.

   **B**  how baseball was invented.

   **C**  when Lou Gehrig played.

   **D**  baseball's Hall of Fame.

2  To find out which book has the most up-to-date information, Cal should look at the —

   **F**  book cover.

   **G**  index.

   **H**  glossary.

   **J**  copyright page.

3  Which is the most likely place to find information about Abner Doubleday, the man who founded the first American baseball league?

   **A**  *Baseball Greats,* Chapter 1

   **B**  *Baseball Greats,* Chapter 3

   **C**  *The History of Baseball,* Chapter 1

   **D**  *The History of Baseball,* Chapter 4

GO ON

**DIRECTIONS**

Darla wants to order a book from the book club at her school. Use the order form to answer questions 4 and 5.

---

**Book Club Order**

Name: **(1)** _____ **(2)** _____
Last                                              First

School: **(3)** _____

Teacher: **(4)** _____

| **(5)** Book Title | **(6)** Quantity | **(7)** Price Each | **(8)** Total Price |
|---|---|---|---|
| | | | |
| | | | |
| | | | |
| | | | |
| | | Grand Total | |

---

**4** On which line should Darla write her teacher's name?

  **F** line 1
  **G** line 2
  **H** line 3
  **J** line 4

**5** Darla wants to buy two copies of the book *1,001 Riddles and Jokes.* In which column should she write the number 2?

  **A** column 5
  **B** column 6
  **C** column 7
  **D** column 8

GO ON ▶

## DIRECTIONS

**Choose the best answer to each question about alphabetical order.**

**6** Which name would be listed first in alphabetical order?

**F** Brown

**G** Burton

**H** Brill

**J** Buck

**7** Which of these names would be listed first in alphabetical order?

**A** Rodney Granger

**B** Chauncey Gardner

**C** Mary Gleason

**D** Syd Gaudier

**8** Shem is making a list of authors in alphabetical order. Which name should come after Margaret Sullivan?

**F** Walter Stargell

**G** May Swenson

**H** Gunther Subic

**J** Angela Sugarman

GO ON

## DIRECTIONS

**Fran Miller has been studying her family's history. She made the time line below. Use the time line to answer questions 9–10.**

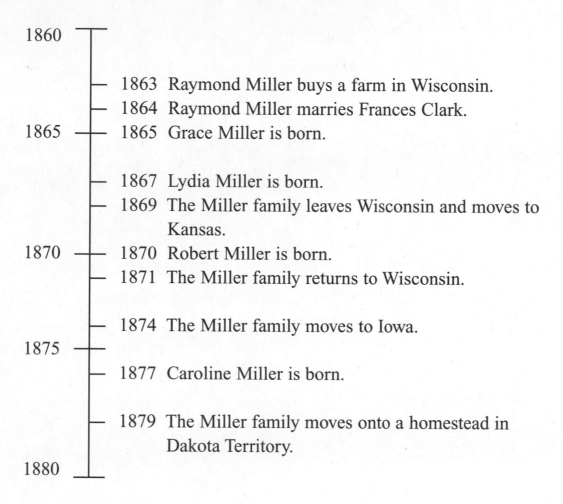

1860

— 1863 Raymond Miller buys a farm in Wisconsin.
— 1864 Raymond Miller marries Frances Clark.
1865 — 1865 Grace Miller is born.

— 1867 Lydia Miller is born.
— 1869 The Miller family leaves Wisconsin and moves to Kansas.
1870 — 1870 Robert Miller is born.
— 1871 The Miller family returns to Wisconsin.

— 1874 The Miller family moves to Iowa.
1875 —

— 1877 Caroline Miller is born.

— 1879 The Miller family moves onto a homestead in Dakota Territory.
1880

**9** In 1874, the Miller family moved to —
A Wisconsin.
B Kansas.
C Iowa.
D Dakota Territory.

**10** Robert Miller was born how many years after Grace was born?
F 2 years
G 5 years
H 10 years
J 15 years

STOP

# Unit 5 Skills Test

## Other Times, Other Places

Name _____

Date _____

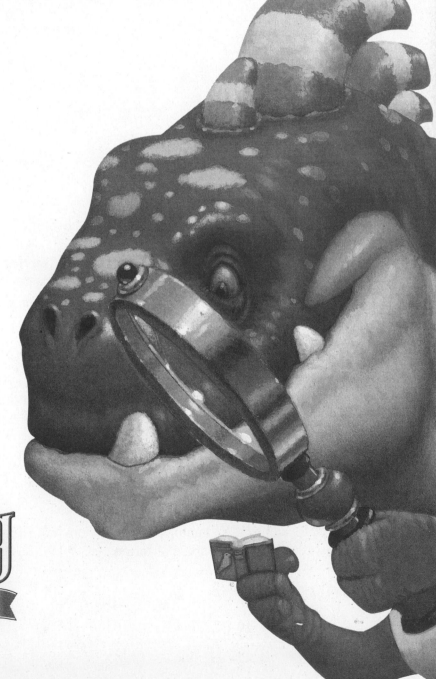

Scott Foresman
Reading
Grade 4

**Editorial Offices**
Glenview, Illinois • New York, New York

**Sales Offices**
Reading, Massachusetts • Duluth, Georgia • Glenview, Illinois
Carrollton, Texas • Menlo Park, California

ISBN 0-673-62432-3

2 3 4 5 6 7 8 9 10-EBA-06  05  04  03  02  01  00

## READING: Comprehension

**DIRECTIONS**

Read each passage. Then read the questions that follow. Choose the best answer to each question. Mark the letter for your answer.

# Back Into Space

Today we are used to the idea that people can travel in space and return safely to Earth. Indeed, astronauts now travel in space so often that many people pay little attention to news stories about them. But things were different on February 20, 1962. On that day, John Glenn became the first American to orbit Earth. Millions of Americans watched on television as Glenn's spaceship was launched. The spaceship circled Earth three times before splashing down in the ocean. Glenn's flight lasted less than five hours, but it made him a hero. All over the United States, newspaper stories praised his skill and courage. When Glenn appeared in parades in New York City and Washington, D.C., huge crowds gathered to cheer him.

However, John Glenn's space flight was just a small step along a long road. The United States wanted to put astronauts on the moon.

Before that could happen, space scientists still had much to learn. The scientists planned other space flights to help them get ready for a moon landing. Many of Glenn's astronaut friends were picked for these flights. Glenn hoped he would get another turn in space too. He waited and waited, but he was always passed over. Finally, Glenn stopped hoping. He gave up his career as an astronaut.

For ten years, Glenn worked as a businessman. Then, in 1974, he became a United States senator from Ohio. Glenn liked being a senator, but after more than twenty years, he decided to retire. He also began thinking about taking another space flight. Glenn went to space scientists with an idea. To learn how being in space affects an older person, Glenn suggested, they could send him into space and measure ways his body changed during the flight. Scientists liked Glenn's idea.

**GO ON** ➡

They asked him to join six other astronauts for a week-long flight on the space shuttle *Discovery*. That is how, on October 29, 1998, at the age of 77, John Glenn's dream of returning to space finally came true.

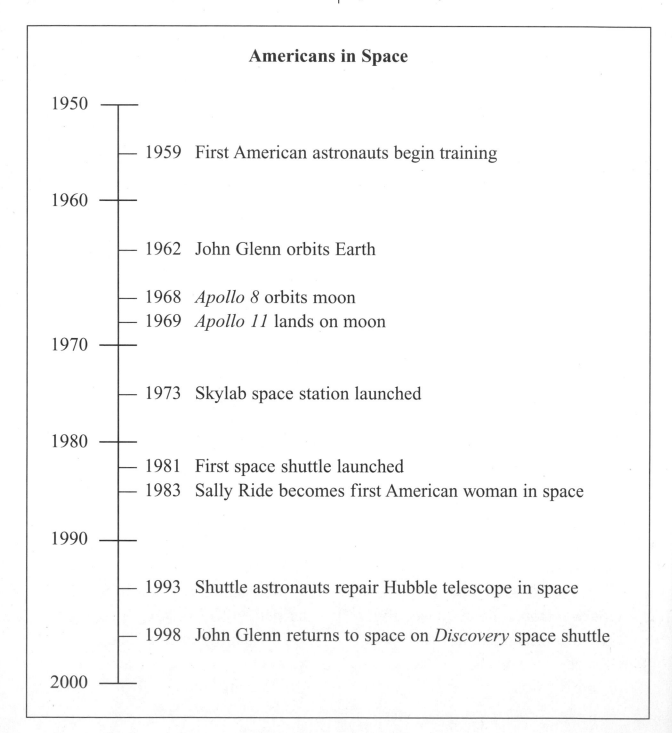

**Americans in Space**

|  |  |
|------|-------|
| 1950 | |
| 1959 | First American astronauts begin training |
| 1960 | |
| 1962 | John Glenn orbits Earth |
| 1968 | *Apollo 8* orbits moon |
| 1969 | *Apollo 11* lands on moon |
| 1970 | |
| 1973 | Skylab space station launched |
| 1980 | |
| 1981 | First space shuttle launched |
| 1983 | Sally Ride becomes first American woman in space |
| 1990 | |
| 1993 | Shuttle astronauts repair Hubble telescope in space |
| 1998 | John Glenn returns to space on *Discovery* space shuttle |
| 2000 | |

GO ON

1 Which is the best summary of this selection?
   A In 1962, John Glenn became the first American to orbit Earth. Thirty-six years later, Glenn returned to space.
   B John Glenn never traveled to the moon, but he became a United States senator.
   C We know that people can travel into space and back. John Glenn did it in 1962.
   D People praised John Glenn as a hero. He made two different trips into space.

2 What kind of selection is this?
   F science fiction
   G realistic fiction
   H narrative nonfiction
   J fantasy

3 Which is a valid generalization based on this selection?
   A Astronauts have boring jobs.
   B Most Americans were very impressed by Glenn's first space flight.
   C Everyone should choose one career and stay with it.
   D Older people should not be astronauts.

4 How long after John Glenn's first flight did *Apollo 11* land on the moon?
   F three years
   G five years
   H seven years
   J ten years

5 In what year was the first space shuttle launched?
   A 1973
   B 1968
   C 1993
   D 1981

6 Most of the information in this selection is presented in —
   F causes and effects.
   G chronological order.
   H problems and solutions.
   J comparison and contrast.

GO ON

# Danger at Niagara Falls

In all of North America, few sights are as beautiful as Niagara Falls. Other waterfalls are higher, but Niagara Falls is the widest and most powerful. People come from all over the world to see and hear its crashing waters.

In the past, there were also those who went to Niagara Falls to do dangerous stunts. Some became famous for their daring, but others were injured or killed when their stunts went wrong.

A man named Jean Francois Gravelet was the most famous person to risk his life doing stunts at Niagara Falls. On a summer day in 1859, Gravelet walked a tightrope across the Niagara River. As graceful as a cat, Gravelet stepped lightly along. He even stopped along the way to take a drink from a bottle! In a later stunt, Gravelet cooked a meal on a small stove while balancing on the tightrope. Another time, he carried a man on his back across the tightrope.

Gravelet was not Niagara Falls's only tightrope walker. There was also Clifford Calverley, who carried a chair to the middle of a tightrope, placed the chair on the rope, and sat down to read a newspaper. Just as daring were the

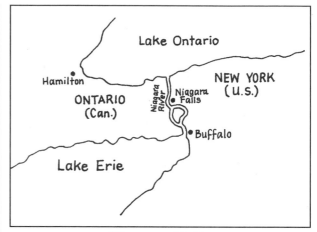

**Niagara Falls**

stunts of Maria Spelterini. She once crossed a tightrope with a blindfold over her eyes. Another time, she crossed a rope wearing a wooden fruit basket on each foot.

Riding over Niagara Falls in a barrel was another stunt that people attempted. A woman named Annie Taylor did it for the first time in 1901. Then for the rest of her life, she tried to make a living by charging Niagara Falls visitors money to hear her story.

Other barrel riders were not as lucky as Annie Taylor. Some died when their barrels crashed into the water, and others were badly injured. It is no wonder that today it is against the law to try dangerous stunts at Niagara Falls. The only safe way to appreciate this powerful waterfall is from a distance.

**GO ON ▶**

**7** Which is the best summary of this selection?

A Niagara Falls is a beautiful sight. It is the widest and most powerful falls in North America.

B People once did many dangerous stunts at Niagara Falls. Now they are only allowed to look at the falls.

C There are many different tightrope-walking stunts that can be done at Niagara Falls.

D Jean Francois Gravelet was the most famous stunt person at Niagara Falls. He did tricks on a tightrope.

**8** The author of this selection presents information about stunts at Niagara Falls by —

F describing events in chronological order.

G giving problems and solutions.

H explaining causes and effects.

J comparing men and women.

**9** In this selection, the author compares Jean Francois Gravelet to a —

A powerful waterfall.

B summer day.

C graceful cat.

D small stove.

**10** You can tell from the map that Niagara Falls is located between —

F Buffalo and Lake Erie.

G New York and Ontario.

H Hamilton and Lake Ontario.

J Hamilton and Lake Erie.

**11** In the final paragraph of this selection, the first two sentences show —

A comparison and contrast.

B cause and effect.

C a question and an answer.

D a problem and a solution.

**12** Which sentence states a generalization?

F "Gravelet walked a tightrope across the Niagara River."

G "Few sights are as beautiful as Niagara Falls."

H "Gravelet was not Niagara Falls's only tightrope walker."

J "A woman named Annie Taylor did it for the first time in 1901."

GO ON

# The Mystery of the Frozen Man

In the fall of 1991, two hikers in the mountains of Italy found a man's body frozen in ice. Police guessed the man might have been a hiker who died thirty or forty years before. To be sure, they brought a doctor to look at the body. Right away, the doctor knew the body was much older than the police guessed.

Who solved the mystery of the frozen man? The body and some objects found with it were turned over to archaeologists, people who study objects from the past. For them, the body and objects were like puzzle pieces. The archaeologists were able to form a picture of the frozen man by fitting the pieces together.

What did archaeologists learn from the body? A test done on the bones showed that the frozen man lived nearly five thousand years ago. Since he had adult teeth, he was probably between twenty-five and forty years old when he died. His leg bones showed that he was more than five feet tall. His head bones showed that he had a large chin and nose and a wide forehead.

How did the frozen man live? The objects found with his body gave some answers. He carried a bow and arrows, probably for hunting animals. He had a

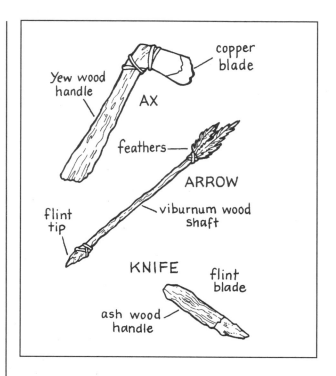

knife, with which he could prepare food. There was an ax, which he might have used to chop wood for fires. There was also a pouch that held two small stones. He may have used these to light fires. Finally, bits of clothing found with the body showed that the frozen man wore animal skins, leather shoes stuffed with grass, a fur cap, and a cape of woven grass.

With the many facts they learned, archaeologists have mostly solved the mystery of the frozen man. However, they still do not know why the frozen man was in the mountains or how he died.

GO ON

**13** What kind of selection is this?

   **A** historical fiction

   **B** expository nonfiction

   **C** fairy tale

   **D** biography

**14** Which is the best summary of this passage?

   **F** A frozen man was found in Italy. Archaeologists learned that the man lived five thousand years ago.

   **G** Archaeologists study clues and put them together like puzzle pieces.

   **H** There were objects near the frozen man. One was an ax he used to chop wood.

   **J** The guess that police made about the frozen man was wrong.

**15** The selection says, "He may have used these to <u>light</u> fires." What does <u>light</u> mean in this sentence?

   **A** not heavy

   **B** to start burning

   **C** not dark

   **D** moving easily

**16** The frozen man's knife and arrows were both made with —

   **F** ash wood.

   **G** copper.

   **H** yew wood.

   **J** flint.

**17** Which is a valid generalization based on this selection?

   **A** Most bodies frozen in the mountains are well preserved.

   **B** Archaeologists will never find another body as old as the frozen man.

   **C** Every person who lived five thousand years ago hunted animals.

   **D** Most archaeologists were excited by the discovery of the frozen man.

**18** Most of the information in this selection is presented as —

   **F** events in chronological order.

   **G** questions and answers.

   **H** events happening from near to far.

   **J** comparison and contrast.

GO ON

# What Happened to Jan?

"Oh, no!" shouted Mr. Palermo. "There's a space creature in the house!"

Jan smiled and waved good-by to her father. Then she walked outside and started down the street. Ever since Scott's invitation arrived, Jan had been working on her costume. She glued small squares of aluminum foil all over a pair of long johns. She sprayed a swim cap with silver paint and tucked her hair inside it. For the final <u>touch</u>, she rubbed green make-up on her face and hands. Now, as she walked to the party, Jan hoped she looked scary.

> ## YOU'RE INVITED
> ## TO A COSTUME PARTY!
>
> Come as someone from the PAST or the FUTURE!
>
> WHERE:  Scott MacDonald's house
>             14 Summit Hill Road
>
> WHEN:  2:00 P.M., Saturday,
>         March 24
>
> PLEASE CALL 555-1563 to say you can come!

"Maybe I'll walk like this," said Jan. She held her arms straight in front of her and let her hands dangle. She took big, stiff steps without bending her knees. Just then a car drove by slowly. The driver stared at Jan, and the children in the back seat pointed. Trying out her space creature face, Jan bared her teeth like an angry dog. The children gasped with fright as the car pulled away. Then two young boys on bikes saw Jan. They jammed on their brakes, made a quick <u>turn</u>, and rode off, yelling, "Let's get out of here!"

Now Jan knew her costume was a success, but she was glad when she got to the party. Everybody there was in a costume too, and no one was afraid of her. Jan was surprised to see so many guests dressed as cave people, knights in armor, explorers, and famous leaders of the past. In fact, Scott was the only other person dressed as a space creature from the future.

"Maybe imagining the future is harder than remembering the past," said Scott.

Jan looked around and nodded. Then she said, "Yes, and a little scary too. Maybe the <u>rest</u> of the guests had the right idea."

**19** Which is the best summary of this passage?

   **A** Scott invited Jan to his costume party.

   **B** Jan walked to a party in the space creature costume she made. Until she got there, everyone who saw her was scared.

   **C** On her way to a party, Jan saw children in a car and on bikes.

   **D** Jan made a costume with aluminum foil, long johns, a swim cap, and paint.

**20** As used in this selection, the word turn means —

   **F** to move around in a circle.

   **G** to spoil or go bad.

   **H** a change in direction.

   **J** a chance to do something.

**21** The author compares Jan's space creature face to the face of —

   **A** a knight in armor.

   **B** a famous leader.

   **C** an angry dog.

   **D** a frightened child.

**22** This selection says, "For the final touch, she rubbed green make-up on her face." What does touch mean in this sentence?

   **F** a detail in a work of art

   **G** to put one's hand on or against

   **H** the sense of feel

   **J** to affect with a feeling

**23** Which is a valid generalization based on this selection?

   **A** Jan had never made a costume before.

   **B** Most guests at the party dressed as someone from the past.

   **C** Scott always has good ideas for parties.

   **D** Everyone loved Jan's costume.

**24** In the last sentence of this selection, rest means —

   **F** sleep.

   **G** to be still.

   **H** to lean or lie against.

   **J** those that are left or remain.

**STOP**

# READING: Word Analysis

**25** Which word means "printed again"?
   A  preprinted
   B  unprinted
   C  misprinted
   D  reprinted

**26** Which word means "opposite of wrap"?
   F  unwrap
   G  rewrap
   H  wrapper
   J  prewrap

**Choose the correct form of the word to complete each sentence.**

**27** We could hear many _____ voices coming from the park.
   A  girls
   B  girl's
   C  girls'
   D  girls's

**28** Two young boys were swinging, and the _____ mother was pushing them.
   F  boys'
   G  boys
   H  boys's
   J  boy's

**Choose the correct way to divide each word into syllables.**

**29** A  un-friend-ly
   B  unf-rien-dly
   C  unfri-end-ly
   D  un-friendl-y

**30** F  rep-ay-ment
   G  re-paym-ent
   H  re-pay-ment
   J  rep-aym-ent

STOP

# WRITING/GRAMMAR

## DIRECTIONS

**Read the passage. Choose the word that best fits in each numbered blank. Mark the letter for your answer.**

---

Last week, Gayle's mother took _____ and Charlie to a car museum.
                                   **(1)**

They looked at the cars, _____ they could not touch anything. The doors of
                          **(2)**

the cars were open, so Gayle and Charlie could see inside _____. When
                                                           **(3)**

Charlie noticed a big crowd, _____ and Gayle hurried into another room.
                              **(4)**

There they saw a car of the future. Gayle said, "I hope this car will be around

for _____ to drive a few years from now."
    **(5)**

---

1  **A**  her
   **B**  she
   **C**  hers
   **D**  she's

2  **F**  but
   **G**  or
   **H**  and
   **J**  nor

3  **A**  it
   **B**  its
   **C**  them
   **D**  they

4  **F**  him
   **G**  himself
   **H**  he
   **J**  his

5  **A**  we
   **B**  us
   **C**  our
   **D**  ourselves

STOP

# WRITING

In this test you have read about John Glenn, Niagara Falls, and the frozen man found in Italy. Choose one of these selections and write a report about it. Use the information in the selection to plan and write your report.

**Prewriting Notes**

GO ON

GO ON

# STUDY SKILLS

## DIRECTIONS

Enrico is writing a report about popular places to visit in the United States. He made these graphs to show some of the information he has learned. Use the graphs to answer questions 1-3.

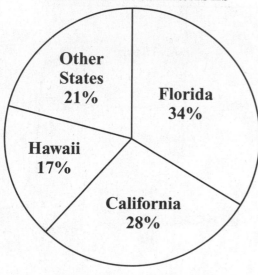

**Americans' Favorite Summer Destinations**

Florida 34%
Other States 21%
Hawaii 17%
California 28%

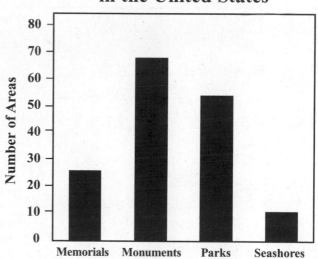

**National Park Service Areas in the United States**

1 California is the favorite summer destination for what percent of travelers?
A 34 %
B 28 %
C 21 %
D 17 %

3 About how many National Park Service areas in the United States are seashores?
A 75
B 55
C 25
D 10

2 The largest percentage of summer travelers like to visit —
F Florida.
G California.
H Hawaii.
J other states.

GO ON

Enrico has found a map showing some interesting places to visit in South Dakota. Use this map to answer questions 4-5.

## SOUTH DAKOTA

0    MILES    80

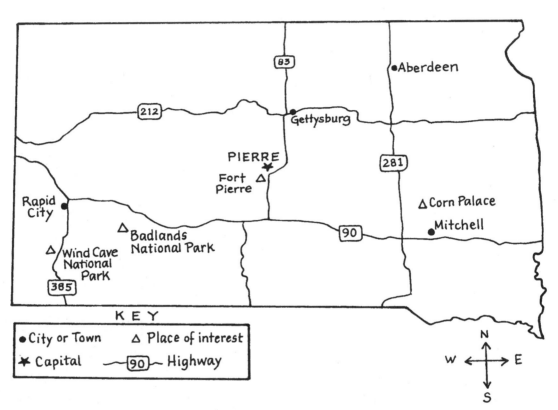

4  The Corn Palace is located outside of which city?
F  Pierre
G  Aberdeen
H  Mitchell
J  Rapid City

5  Wind Cave National Park is located along which highway?
A  Route 90
B  Route 281
C  Route 212
D  Route 385

STOP

# Unit 6 Skills Test

## Express Yourself!

Name _____

Date _____

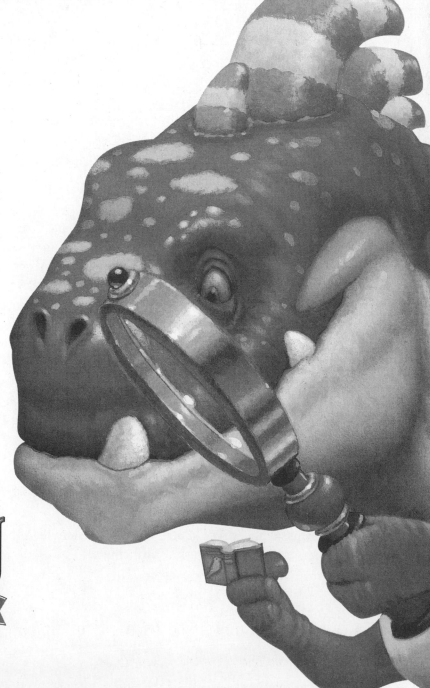

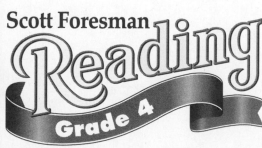
Scott Foresman Reading
Grade 4

**Editorial Offices**
Glenview, Illinois • New York, New York

**Sales Offices**
Reading, Massachusetts • Duluth, Georgia • Glenview, Illinois
Carrollton, Texas • Menlo Park, California

ISBN 0-673-62433-1

2 3 4 5 6 7 8 9 10-EBA-06 05 04 03 02 01 00

# READING: Comprehension

**DIRECTIONS**
Read each passage. Then read the questions that follow. Choose the best answer to each question. Mark the letter for your answer.

# What's Behind a Movie?

Making a movie is complicated. It all starts with the producer. The producer is the boss who is in charge of the business of making a movie.

The producer's first step is deciding what film to make. Many films are based on stories that were first told in books. Once a story is picked, the producer hires a screenwriter to rewrite the story for the screen. The producer also hires a director. The director is in charge of the art of moviemaking.

Then it's time to select the actors. Producers love to hire famous actors because the public will pay to see a film starring these people. Still, stars are expensive. That's why a film usually has some famous performers and some who are not so famous.

A movie is a series of shots. It might begin with a shot of a door. The next shot could show the door opening and a boy running out. The third shot might show a monster running after the boy! To save time and money, every shot in a movie is planned before filming begins. The detailed plan is called a storyboard. It is a set of small pictures and looks almost like a comic book. There may be a thousand storyboards for just one movie!

The actors are hired, the script is written, and the storyboard is finished. Can the cameras finally start to roll?

Not yet. Some movies are filmed in real places, while others are filmed on giant stages. A film set might show the inside of a spaceship or a castle from long ago. Building a set is a lot of work, and so is the making of costumes for the actors to wear. In many movies, actors require make-up to make them

**GO ON**

look old or injured or different in some way. Putting on this make-up every day can take a long time.

**How to Make An Actor Look Old**

1. Give the actor a gray wig.
2. Put pale make-up all over the actor's face.
3. Use darker make-up to darken the shadows under the actor's eyes.
4. Make shadows under the actor's cheeks with make-up.
5. Use a fine pencil to draw wrinkles around the actor's eyes.

Finally, filming begins. The actors go on the set wearing their costumes and make-up. Excitement fills the air. Getting a scene right can take many tries, so being an actor can sometimes be frustrating.

After every scene has been filmed, the final movie is put together, which is kind of like polishing the rough draft of a paper. An editor takes all the bits of film and combines them into a smoothly flowing story. Then a composer writes music to go along with the pictures that appear on the screen.

Next time you see a movie, think of all the work that went into it!

GO ON

1 What is the main idea of this selection?
   A  Many actors are expensive to hire.
   B  Making a movie is complicated.
   C  The producer is the most important person in making a movie.
   D  It takes a long time to make actors look old.

2 Which detail from the selection best supports the main idea?
   F  "Producers love to hire famous actors."
   G  "There may be a thousand storyboards for just one movie!"
   H  "Some movies are filmed in real places."
   J  "Still, stars are expensive."

3 The author's main purpose in this selection is to —
   A  entertain the reader with funny stories from the movies.
   B  persuade readers to try a career in the movies.
   C  inform readers about how movies are made.
   D  describe what a day on a movie set feels like.

4 Which of these steps takes place after a movie is filmed?
   F  The composer writes music.
   G  The storyboard is created.
   H  The director is hired.
   J  The set is built.

5 What kind of selection is this?
   A  biography
   B  historical fiction
   C  narrative nonfiction
   D  advertisement

6 Which statement from this selection is an opinion?
   F  "Every shot in a movie is planned before filming begins."
   G  "The detailed plan is called a storyboard."
   H  "A movie is a series of shots."
   J  "Making a movie is complicated."

GO ON

# Gutenberg's Great Invention

Today books are everywhere. They fill the shelves of homes, schools, libraries, and supermarkets. Six hundred years ago, however, most people had never even seen a book. At that time, most books were written out by hand. It took a long time to letter each page, so books were expensive and rare.

Then a man named Johannes Gutenberg changed the world. He invented a machine that could print books.

Johannes Gutenberg was a German craftsman. He had a small business making mirrors and cheap jewelry. He also had a secret dream. He wanted to design a machine to print words. In his spare time, he tried to make such a machine.

He started by making letters of the alphabet out of lead. If he covered the letters with ink and then pressed them down on paper, they left a letter-shaped mark. However, pressing them down by hand was slow and clumsy. Gutenberg wanted to invent a machine that could press the letters onto paper.

Around 1448, Gutenberg printed several copies of a famous book. Some people who saw Gutenberg's copies got excited. They realized that printing was a way of making books available to more people. Most people, however, were not impressed. They thought the old, handmade books were much better than Gutenberg's.

Gutenberg kept finding ways to improve his press. Still, he kept having money trouble. To keep going, he needed molds, ink, special cleaners, metals, brushes, brooms, and many other supplies.

In 1455, Gutenberg began to print a Bible. He printed about two hundred copies. The pages were very clear and beautiful. Today these books are famous throughout the world. Before his death in 1468, Gutenberg also printed an encyclopedia and a calendar. He trained many young workers to become printers as well. By 1500, there were over a thousand printers in Europe! Books were no longer for just a few rich or special people. Thanks to Gutenberg, books were <u>inexpensive</u> enough for millions of people to buy and read!

GO ON

**7** What is the main idea of this passage?

  **A** Gutenberg found a way to invent a printing press that changed the world.

  **B** Gutenberg had a lot of trouble with money.

  **C** Gutenberg started out as a maker of jewelry.

  **D** Gutenberg lived a long time ago.

**8** Which sentence states an opinion?

  **F** "Most people had never even seen a book."

  **G** "Johannes Gutenberg was a German craftsman."

  **H** "He had a small business making mirrors and cheap jewelry."

  **J** "The pages were very clear and beautiful."

**9** What kind of selection is this?

  **A** folk tale

  **B** realistic fiction

  **C** advertisement

  **D** biography

**10** Which sentence states a fact?

  **F** "In 1454, Gutenberg began to print a Bible."

  **G** "These books are famous throughout the world."

  **H** "Most people, however, were not impressed."

  **J** "The old, handmade books were much better."

**11** The author's main purpose in this passage is to —

  **A** entertain with a story about books.

  **B** persuade readers to buy books.

  **C** give information about Gutenberg.

  **D** compare Gutenberg's books with handwritten books.

**12** In this passage, the word inexpensive means —

  **F** large.

  **G** clear.

  **H** cheap.

  **J** pretty.

GO ON ➡

# Raising an Unusual Pet

Usually when you raise a pet, you keep it for its whole life. Raising a monarch butterfly is different. You watch it develop from a wriggling caterpillar to a creature with wings. Then it's time to say good-by.

The first step in raising this unusual pet is to find some eggs. The best time to look is usually in spring or early summer. Find some milkweed plants growing in a field or beside a road. Then watch for an orange-and-black monarch butterfly. If one lands on a milkweed leaf and then flies away, look underneath the leaf. If the butterfly has deposited a small, whitish egg, remove the leaf and bring it inside.

Dampen a paper towel and place it on a foil plate. Put the leaf on the plate, and then cover the plate with a plastic bag to keep the leaf from drying out. In one to four days, a baby caterpillar will hatch.

Keep the caterpillar inside the plastic bag for a week. Make sure the bag is puffed out with air so that the caterpillar can breathe. Keep your little pet supplied with fresh milkweed leaves. The caterpillar will eat constantly and grow quickly.

After a week, put the caterpillar in a large glass jar. Add a stem covered with milkweed leaves. Cover the jar with a screen so your pet can breathe but not escape.

For the next few weeks, you will have fun watching the caterpillar grow. From time to time, it will wriggle out of its old, too-small skin, just as a snake does. When it is fully grown, the monarch caterpillar attaches itself to a twig. Its skin splits for the last time, and a green blob appears. At first the blob is soft, but then it hardens. This is the chrysalis, a case inside which the caterpillar enters its last stage of growth.

The chrysalis hangs on the twig for nine to fourteen days. Don't forget to check your pet during this time period. The chrysalis will become transparent. You will see orange and black wings inside. Soon the shell will crack and split open. Out will come the butterfly, its wings damp and wrinkled.

Watch as the butterfly's wings dry and then open. Then let the butterfly rest in its jar overnight. Set it free outside the next morning. For a few minutes it will probably circle around you. Then it will sail off.

The next time you see a monarch butterfly sipping nectar from a flower, you may wonder: Is that the pet I raised?

GO ON ▶

**13** What is this passage mostly about?

   **A** deciding what kind of pet to raise

   **B** raising a pet for its whole life

   **C** identifying different types of butterflies

   **D** raising a monarch butterfly

**14** Which sentence states an opinion?

   **F** "The caterpillar will eat constantly and grow quickly."

   **G** "For the next few weeks, you will have fun watching the caterpillar grow."

   **H** "At first the blob is soft, but then it hardens."

   **J** "The chrysalis hangs on the twig for nine to fourteen days."

**15** Which is the first step in finding monarch butterfly eggs?

   **A** looking for milkweed plants

   **B** covering the plate with a plastic bag

   **C** filling a bag with air

   **D** putting the leaf on a plate

**16** What kind of selection is this?

   **F** biography

   **G** folk tale

   **H** expository nonfiction

   **J** realistic fiction

**17** The author's main purpose in this passage is to —

   **A** express feelings about butterflies.

   **B** entertain with a story about a butterfly.

   **C** persuade readers to take care of pets.

   **D** explain the process of raising a butterfly.

**18** In this passage, the word deposited means —

   **F** looked closely at.

   **G** removed; taken away.

   **H** kept damp.

   **J** put down; left lying.

**GO ON**

# HAVE A PUPPET PARTY WITH PAULA THE PUPPETEER

Is your birthday coming up soon? What kind of party do you want to have: a dull, boring, ORDINARY birthday party, or one that is wild, crazy, and FUN? If you want to have a great time and <u>astonish</u> your guests, get Paula the Puppeteer to run your party.

Paula is no ordinary puppeteer. Years ago she learned the art of puppets from Madame Claire, the greatest puppeteer of all. Now Paula is a puppet master! She owns every kind of puppet in the world—sock puppets, glove puppets, paper bag puppets, stick puppets. She creates characters you'll recognize from books and movies. She can work up to ten puppets at a time. Her puppets don't just bob their heads up and down behind a silly cardboard stage. They come out into the room and perform for you. They dance, in-line skate, and set off fireworks—not scary fireworks with real fire, but yummy safe displays made of whipped cream and red-hot candies! You won't believe your eyes!

Paula's puppets will be the center of the party for every amazing minute. First they'll meet the guests at the door and lead the party games. Next they'll serve the cake and ice cream and lead the singing of "Happy Birthday!" Then they'll <u>challenge</u> guests to the world's trickiest treasure hunt and hand out wonderful party bags when the fun is over. Finally, they'll even clean up the house after everybody leaves. You'll be able to play with your new toys.

Paula and her puppets make real party magic. Even your parents will love Paula. The charge for a puppet party is only $75.00. To have Paula for your party, call 555-6024.

GO ON

**19** What do Paula's puppets do first at a party?

  **A** meet the guests at the door

  **B** set off whipped-cream fireworks

  **C** go out into the room and perform

  **D** serve ice cream

**20** In this passage, challenge means —

  **F** invite to a game or contest.

  **G** argue with.

  **H** show off.

  **J** give gifts to.

**21** What is the last step in one of Paula's puppet parties?

  **A** serving the cake

  **B** meeting the guests at the door

  **C** cleaning up the house

  **D** handing out party bags

**22** The author's main purpose in this passage is to —

  **F** entertain you with a story about puppets.

  **G** explain how to make different kinds of puppets.

  **H** describe what it feels like to operate a puppet.

  **J** persuade you to hire Paula for your party.

**23** The writer of this selection mentions an event from the past to —

  **A** describe the puppets Paula owns.

  **B** explain how Paula learned the art of puppets.

  **C** describe what the fireworks are made of.

  **D** explain what will happen during the party.

**24** In this passage, the word astonish means —

  **F** warn.

  **G** amaze.

  **H** cheer.

  **J** welcome.

STOP

# READING: Word Analysis

**DIRECTIONS**

Choose the correct plural form of the word that fits in the blank. Mark the letter for your answer.

**25** Three _____ jumped over the gate.

    **A** sheepes

    **B** sheeps

    **C** sheepies

    **D** sheep

**26** Dad found five _____ in the garage.

    **F** meese

    **G** mouses

    **H** mice

    **J** mousies

**27** Six _____ went to the meeting.

    **A** women

    **B** woman

    **C** womans

    **D** womens

**DIRECTIONS**

Choose the correct spelling of the word when the suffix is added to the base word.

**28** explain + -ation =

    **F** explaintion

    **G** explanation

    **H** explaination

    **J** explannation

**29** maintain + -ance =

    **A** maintainance

    **B** maintance

    **C** maintenance

    **D** maintainnance

**30** describe + -tion =

    **F** describetion

    **G** describation

    **H** describtion

    **J** description

STOP

# WRITING/GRAMMAR

## DIRECTIONS

Read each passage. Some parts are underlined. The underlined parts may contain mistakes in punctuation or may be written incorrectly. Mark the letter beside the best way to write each underlined part. If the underlined part needs no change, mark the choice "No mistake."

---

Last night I got a phone call from my aunt who lives in Mobile Alabama.
**(1)**

She asked, "Natalie would you like to go to a concert with me?" She said
**(2)**

the concert would be a program of songs that were originally sung by

slaves.

---

**1 A** my aunt who lives in Mobile, Alabama?

**B** my aunt who lives in Mobile, Alabama.

**C** my aunt who lives in Mobile Alabama!

**D** No mistake

**2 F** "Natalie? would you like to go to the concert with me."

**G** "Natalie would you like to go to a concert with me."

**H** "Natalie, would you like to go to a concert with me?"

**J** No mistake

GO ON

I couldn't help staring as Darrell heaved his stack of books onto the counter so the librarian could check them out. <u>He had books on carpentry,</u>
(3)

<u>computers crocodiles and crafts.</u> I was amazed. <u>What a pile of books he had!</u>
(4)

I asked him, <u>How will you ever read all those books?</u>
(5)

3  A  He had books on carpentry computers crocodiles, and crafts.

   B  He had books on carpentry, computers, crocodiles, and, crafts.

   C  He had books on carpentry, computers, crocodiles, and crafts.

   D  No mistake

4  F  What a pile of books he had?

   G  What a pile of books he had,

   H  "What a pile of books he had!"

   J  No mistake

5  A  "How will you ever read all those books?"

   B  How will you ever read all those books.

   C  "How will you ever read all those books,"

   D  No mistake

STOP

# WRITING

Imagine that your school has some extra money to spend. Do you think the school should spend the money to improve the art and music programs or to buy new computers?

Write a persuasive argument to state your opinion. Give reasons and details to support your view.

**Prewriting Notes**

GO ON

GO ON

STOP

# STUDY SKILLS

**DIRECTIONS**
Use the poster below to answer questions 1 and 2.

### The Pioneer Valley Dance Company
### Presents

### *CINDERELLA*

**Friday, March 5**
6:30 P.M.
**Sherman Elementary School**
**Sherman, Connecticut**

**Saturday, March 6**
1:00 P.M.
**Old Harbor Middle School**
**Monroe, Connecticut**

**Saturday, March 6**
7:00 P.M.
**Town Hall**
**West Banford, Connecticut**

**Sunday, March 7**
3:00 P.M.
**Merry Vale Day School**
**Old Tyme, Connecticut**

Tickets: $4.00 children, $6.00 adults
**KIDS FOUR AND UNDER GET IN FREE!**

**1**  Where will the Friday show be
presented?

    **A**  Sherman Elementary School

    **B**  West Banford Town Hall

    **C**  Old Harbor Middle School

    **D**  Merry Vale Day School

**2**  At what time is the second show on
March 6?

    **F**  1:00 P.M.

    **G**  3:00 P.M.

    **H**  6:30 P.M.

    **J**  7:00 P.M.

GO ON

# DIRECTIONS

**Use this part of a page from a dictionary to answer questions 3–5.**

---

**flavor ■ flight¹**

**fla·vor** (flā′vər), **1** *n.* taste, especially a particular taste: *Chocolate and vanilla have different flavors.* **2** *v.* to give added taste to; season: *The onion flavors the whole stew.* **3** *n.* flavoring. **4** *n.* a special quality: *Stories about ships have a flavor of the sea.* —**fla′vor·less,** *adj.*

**fla·vor·ful** (flā′vər fəl), *adj.* having flavor and interest. ■ See Synonym Study at **tasty.**

**fla·vor·ing** (flā′vər ing), *n.* something used to give a particular taste to food or drink: *chocolate flavoring.*

**flaw** (flô), **1** *n.* a slight defect; fault; blemish: *A flaw in the dish caused it to break. A quick temper is a character flaw.* **2** *v.* to make or become defective: *A tiny chip flawed the diamond.*

**flaw·less** (flô′lis), *adj.* without a flaw; perfect: *The actor's performance was flawless.* —**flaw′less·ly,** *adv.* —**flaw′less·ness,** *n.*

**flax** (flaks), *n.* **1** a slender, upright plant with small, narrow leaves, blue flowers, and slender stems. Linseed oil is made from its seeds. **2** the threadlike parts into which the stems of this plant separate. Flax is spun into thread and woven into linen.

**flax·en** (flak′sən), *adj.* **1** made of flax. **2** like the color of flax; pale yellow: *Flaxen hair is very light.*

**flay** (flā), *v.* **1** to strip off the skin or outer covering of. **2** to scold severely; criticize without pity or mercy. —**flay′er,** *n.*

---

**3** How many syllables are in the word flavorful?

A two

B three

C four

D five

**4** In which word is the *a* pronounced the same as the *a* in flavor?

F flaw

G flaxen

H flawless

J flay

**5** Which of these words could also appear on this page of the dictionary?

A flex

B floor

C flit

D flame

# End-of-Year Skills Test

Name _____

Date _____

Scott Foresman
Reading
Grade 4

**Editorial Offices**
Glenview, Illinois • New York, New York

**Sales Offices**
Reading, Massachusetts • Duluth, Georgia • Glenview, Illinois
Carrollton, Texas • Menlo Park, California

ISBN 0-673-62449-8

2 3 4 5 6 7 8 9 10-EBA-06  05  04  03  02  01  00

# READING: Comprehension

**DIRECTIONS**

Read each passage. Then read the questions that follow. Choose the best answer to each question. Mark the letter for your answer.

# Braving the Waves

Ramona was nervous. She tightened her life jacket and tried to get comfortable. The sailboat was a catamaran. It had two thin hulls joined by metal bars that also held up a canvas platform. Ramona sat on the platform and took the tiller in her hand. This was her first chance to sail her uncle's boat by herself. Her uncle wanted her to feel confident about sailing alone, and she didn't want to make any mistakes. The wind was strong, and the waves on the Gulf of Mexico were deep and even. Her uncle watched on the dock.

Ramona went through a checklist in her mind. Quickly she looked up at the sail. It was tight and smooth. She had the lines in order, and everything was tied down.

She gave a cheery wave to her uncle, hoping it would make her look less nervous than she felt. Then she pushed the boat away from the dock, slid the tiller to one side, and tightened the line that set the sail. The boat moved smartly away from the dock, humming as it cut through the salty water.

"I'm sailing!" Ramona said to herself. "I'm really sailing!"

The catamaran cut across the water, picking up speed. Ramona turned the boat farther away from the wind, and it went faster still. Then, slowly, one of the hulls lifted out of the water. At first it rose just a little, still splashing the tops of the waves. Then it went a bit higher, clearing the water altogether.

"I'm flying a hull!" Ramona laughed. "I've always wanted to do that!"

GO ON ➡

She was sure that she looked great from the dock. The boat, with its brightly colored sail and blue hulls, would stand out against the green water as it flew along. Ramona grinned and started to relax.

That's when it happened. The hull that was still in the water caught a wave, the front end wedging into the water. The sailboat flipped forward. Ramona flew through the air and landed in the water with a splash.

When she had bobbed up to the surface and wiped the salty water from her eyes, she saw that her uncle's boat was upside down.

"Oh, no!" she thought. "He's going to be so angry!"

She had a lot of practice in turning a boat over, so she got to work. She pulled a <u>line</u> over one hull and stood on the other, pulling hard against the rope. The boat slowly righted itself as Ramona eased back into the water. She climbed back up onto the catamaran and sailed it—slowly—back to the dock.

But instead of being angry, her uncle simply smiled. He told her to tie the boat securely to the dock and come up to the house for dinner.

"You're not upset?" Ramona asked.

Her uncle shook his head. "No, sweetheart," he said. "You never know how far a boat can lean before going over—until you flip one."

GO ON

1  What is the theme of this story?
   A  Some people never learn from their mistakes.
   B  The best way to learn about something is to do it.
   C  Life is too short to worry all the time.
   D  Learning should always be fun.

2  Which word best describes Ramona's uncle when she returns to the dock?
   F  upset
   G  worried
   H  disappointed
   J  understanding

3  What kind of selection is this?
   A  historical fiction
   B  mystery
   C  realistic fiction
   D  folk tale

4  In this passage, the word <u>line</u> means —
   F  a rope, cord, or wire.
   G  a long, narrow mark.
   H  to arrange in a row.
   J  a row of words on a page.

5  Which sentence best helps you picture in your mind what the boat looks like?
   A  "Ramona turned the boat farther away from the wind, and it went faster still."
   B  "The hull that was still in the water caught a wave."
   C  "The boat slowly righted itself as Ramona eased back into the water."
   D  "The boat, with its brightly colored sail and blue hulls, would stand out against the green water as it flew along."

GO ON

# World Food Day Schedule

Jefferson School's World Food Day will be held this Tuesday in the lunchroom. The classes from each grade will make food from one continent. Each class will prepare its dish Tuesday morning. Everyone will get to sample all the dishes. Classes will go to the lunchroom at the times listed below.

Students will dress in costumes from the countries they represent. Student art will cover the walls. In addition, Mr. Maser's music group will play several songs on steel drums and marimbas.

This event was Mr. Chan's idea. He wanted to start a school tradition in which everyone came together to see the diversity and richness of the world around us. The other teachers liked the idea. They spoke with their students about it. The students also liked the idea and were happy to do the work.

On Tuesday, remember to wear your costume. Bring a drink from home, if you like, or plan to buy milk. Be sure to bring along your appetite.

| Grade | Teacher | Lunch Dish | Time |
| --- | --- | --- | --- |
| 1 | Ms. Hanratty | Pad tai (Thailand) | 11:20 A.M. |
| 1 | Mr. Guillermo | Fish tempura (Japan) | 11:25 A.M. |
| 2 | Ms. Walker | Bratwurst (Germany) | 11:30 A.M. |
| 2 | Mr. Won | Crepes (France) | 11:35 A.M. |
| 3 | Ms. Reynold | Corn fritters (U.S.) | 11:40 A.M. |
| 3 | Ms. Beck | Capelin chowder (Canada) | 11:45 A.M. |
| 4 | Ms. Orejuela | Bean tortillas (Brazil) | 11:50 A.M. |
| 4 | Ms. Thatcher | Molé (Peru) | 11:55 A.M. |
| 5 | Mr. Chan | Grilled shrimp (Australia) | 12:00 NOON |
| 5 | Ms. Weaver | Mutton stew (Australia) | 12:05 P.M. |
| 6 | Ms. Prefontaine | Mango chutney (Mali) | 12:10 P.M. |
| 6 | Mr. Harper | Candied yams (Malawi) | 12:15 P.M. |

Thank you to all the teachers and students who made this event possible. Everyone's help is appreciated.

GO ON

**6** What will students do when they go to the lunchroom on Tuesday at the scheduled time?

    **F** put up art work

    **G** make a special dish

    **H** put on costumes

    **J** sample all the dishes

**7** At what time should Ms. Thatcher's class arrive in the lunchroom on Tuesday?

    **A** 11:20 A.M.

    **B** 11:55 A.M.

    **C** 12:00 NOON

    **D** 12:15 P.M.

**8** The fifth graders are preparing dishes from —

    **F** Japan.

    **G** France.

    **H** North America.

    **J** Australia.

**9** Jefferson School's World Food Day was planned because —

    **A** several teachers decided to do all the work.

    **B** Mr. Maser taught a group of students to play steel drums and marimbas.

    **C** students wanted to try some new foods in the lunchroom.

    **D** students and teachers liked Mr. Chan's idea to start a school tradition.

**10** If this World Food Day is a success, what will likely happen next year?

    **F** Another World Food Day will be held.

    **G** People from other countries will be invited to lunch.

    **H** All the dishes will be made at home and brought to the lunchroom.

    **J** Students will take field trips to other countries.

STOP

# How to Record Your Family's Oral History

Do you remember when the tornado hit? Do you know the story of how your parents met? How did they decide to name their children? Every family has stories, and these stories can be precious treasures. But most people never record their family's stories, and eventually most tales are forgotten.

To save the stories that your family tells, all you need is a tape recorder, some paper, the interest, and the time. Begin with older members of your family who live in your house or nearby. Your grandmother, for example, might help you get the project going well. Explain to her what you are doing and ask her to talk with you for an hour or so. Let her know the kinds of things you want to talk about so she has time to think about them and remember the stories she would like to tell.

Before you begin, make sure you have everything ready. You will need a tape recorder. Check to make sure it is working well and has fresh batteries. Have several blank tapes handy as well. Also prepare a list of questions in advance. Make sure you can do the interview in a comfortable, quiet place. The subject's home is often best.

To start the interview, turn on the recorder and state your name, the name of the person you are interviewing, and the date. Then relax and begin asking your questions. Let the person speak as long as he or she wishes, and don't worry if the conversation strays from your list of questions.

Limit the session to an hour or so. You don't want your subject to get tired or bored with the project. When you are done, thank your subject and promise to give him or her a written copy of the interview.

At home, listen to the tape and type or write everything that was said. Don't bother trying to fix any grammatical mistakes or other errors; people will want to "hear" your subject's own way of speaking when they read the interview later.

Make several copies of the written transcript, and keep some of them along with the tape in a safe place. Bind the rest into booklets that can be mailed to the other members of your family. They will enjoy and appreciate these gems for years to come.

GO ON

**11** What is the main idea of this passage?

- **A** Recording a family's history requires a lot of work.
- **B** Oral histories are valuable and easy to create.
- **C** Oral histories must follow strict rules.
- **D** A family's history should begin with grandparents.

**12** The information in this passage is presented mainly as a series of —

- **F** comparisons and contrasts.
- **G** causes and effects.
- **H** problems and solutions.
- **J** steps in a process.

**13** According to the author of this passage, when you thank your subject for the interview, you should also —

- **A** explain what you are doing.
- **B** promise to provide a written copy of the interview.
- **C** prepare a list of questions.
- **D** check to make sure your recorder is working.

**14** Which is a valid generalization based on the passage?

- **F** Family stories can be precious treasures to family members.
- **G** Family stories are always forgotten.
- **H** Family stories are usually silly.
- **J** Family stories are written and saved by most families.

**15** In this passage, the word <u>transcript</u> means —

- **A** a thank-you note.
- **B** a tape.
- **C** a written copy.
- **D** a booklet.

GO ON

# The Gulf Stream

You're sailing across the easy waves of the Atlantic Ocean, maybe just a few miles off the coast of Georgia. Some dolphins dance nearby, keeping pace with your boat. A stingray cuts through the water just below the surface. The sun is shining warm and bright. It is a beautiful day.

But ahead, you see something strange. It is like a stair-step in the water, a kind of wave that doesn't seem to move. As you sail into it, your boat jumps upward and turns sharply to the north. You have reached the Gulf Stream. First named by Benjamin Franklin, this strong current of water curls up from the South Atlantic and brings warm water and nutrients to the North Atlantic and across to Ireland.

Two warm currents of water from the Gulf of Mexico come together to make the Gulf Stream. The Gulf Stream brings some of the sun's warmth to the cold North Atlantic. It keeps Newfoundland warm and foggy, even while areas farther from the shore are clear and cold. It makes it easier to sail east in the North Atlantic, but it pushes against boats trying to sail west.

The Gulf Stream carries so much water that it often rises several feet above the surrounding ocean level. The water in the Gulf Stream is often saltier and more heavily laden with food, oxygen, and silt than is the water to either side. Without the Gulf Stream, many ocean animals would have great difficulty living in the otherwise barren waters of the North Atlantic.

The Gulf Stream is part of one of many systems that stir up our planet. Like weather systems in the sky, the Gulf Stream mixes the elements around it, keeping everything moving and preventing dangerous imbalances. Without the Gulf Stream, life on Earth would be very different—and, in places, very difficult indeed.

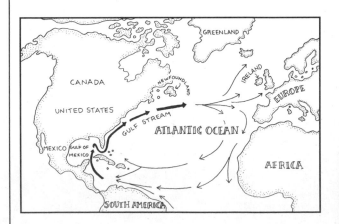

**16** How is water in the Gulf Stream different from the water around it?

   **F**  It has less oxygen and silt.

   **G**  It is colder.

   **H**  It is saltier and has more nutrients.

   **J**  It is cleaner.

**17** According to the passage, ocean currents are like weather systems because they —

   **A**  cause rain and clouds.

   **B**  mix things up and even out imbalances.

   **C**  carry nutrients and silt.

   **D**  change from one minute to the next.

**18** From the map, you can tell that after the Gulf Stream reaches Europe it —

   **F**  flows south toward Africa.

   **G**  flows along the east coast of the United States.

   **H**  moves toward Greenland.

   **J**  moves north toward Canada.

**19** The author's purpose in this passage is to —

   **A**  persuade readers to sail the Gulf Stream.

   **B**  entertain readers with an amusing story about sailing the Gulf Stream.

   **C**  describe the creatures that live in the Gulf Stream.

   **D**  inform readers about the Gulf Stream.

**20** What kind of selection is this?

   **F**  expository nonfiction

   **G**  folk tale

   **H**  realistic fiction

   **J**  biography

**GO ON**

# With the New Sloink, Every Day Is Funday!

Most balls bounce and most balls roll, but the Sloink fills hours with fun. The Sloink is a bouncy red ball covered with lively silver springs. When you throw it, it bounces higher than any other ball you can buy. When you roll it, it worms across the floor. People can't get enough of the Sloink!

*"I haven't had this much fun in years!"—Adam, Grade 4*

*"The most fun I've ever had with a bouncy ball!"—Jill, Grade 3*

*"It makes me laugh so hard my sides hurt!"—Joachim, Grade 4*

The Sloink ball has been tested by three laboratories. It has bounced more than eight feet high. In one case, it bounced six times. Each bounce sent the ball over the heads of the researchers! The Sloink has also passed all U.S. toy safety tests. It is safe, nontoxic, and will last for years.

Sloink's secret lies in the special metals used to make its springs. They are made of a titanium alloy that returns more than 95 percent of the energy it receives. These springs are among the bounciest ever made. In fact, NASA may use Sloink springs to cushion delicate machines on the next Space Shuttle mission.

But mainly, the Sloink is pure, simple fun. You can skip it across a hard surface and make it bounce several times on its way to your friend. You can bounce it from the floor to the wall and back to the floor, making it zig-zag its way across the room. Sloink masters can even juggle up to seven Sloinks at a time, using their springy action to keep the balls moving at high speeds.

So get a Sloink today. You'll still love playing with it decades from now.

GO ON

**21** The author of this passage mainly wants readers to —

  **A** bounce Sloinks off the walls and floor.

  **B** give their Sloinks to NASA.

  **C** learn how to juggle.

  **D** buy Sloinks for themselves.

**22** Which sentence states an opinion?

  **F** "Sloink's secret lies in the special metals used to make its springs."

  **G** "But mainly, the Sloink is pure, simple fun."

  **H** "You can skip it across a hard surface and make it bounce several times on its way to your friend."

  **J** "Sloink masters can even juggle up to seven Sloinks at a time."

**23** The author of this passage thinks people will enjoy the Sloink mainly because it —

  **A** bounces high and rolls wildly.

  **B** will last a long time.

  **C** is covered with special titanium springs.

  **D** is a new invention.

**24** The quotations from children are most likely included in the ad to —

  **F** prove that the Sloink is brand new.

  **G** describe what the Sloink looks like.

  **H** prove that the Sloink bounces high.

  **J** convince readers that the Sloink is fun.

**25** Which sentence best helps you visualize what a Sloink looks like?

  **A** "Most balls bounce and most balls roll."

  **B** "It bounces higher than any other ball you can buy."

  **C** "The Sloink is a bouncy red ball covered with lively silver springs."

  **D** "People can't get enough of the Sloink!"

**STOP**

# READING: Word Analysis

## DIRECTIONS
Choose the best answer to each question. Mark the letter for your answer.

1 What is the prefix in the word misspelled?
   A mis
   B spell
   C miss
   D ed

2 Which word means "opposite of written"?
   F rewritten
   G miswritten
   H unwritten
   J prewritten

3 What is the suffix in the word encouragement?
   A en
   B courage
   C ent
   D ment

4 Which word means "without pain"?
   F painful
   G painless
   H painfully
   J painfulness

GO ON

## DIRECTIONS

**Choose the correct form of the word to complete each sentence.**
**Mark the letter for your answer.**

**5** Mr. Kline _____ kids how to use computers.
- **A** teachs
- **B** teach
- **C** teaches
- **D** teaching

**6** Why did all the students put their sneakers on the wrong _____?
- **F** foot
- **G** foots
- **H** feets
- **J** feet

**7** Lisa put flowers in all four of her _____ rooms.
- **A** brothers'
- **B** brother
- **C** brother's
- **D** brothers

**8** Jeff _____ red and yellow paints to make orange.
- **F** mixes
- **G** mix
- **H** mixs
- **J** mixxes

**9** I can hardly wait to see my all _____ faces when I tell them.
- **A** friends
- **B** friends'
- **C** friends's
- **D** friend's

**10** Tracy made a flag with stripes of three different _____.
- **F** color
- **G** colores
- **H** colors
- **J** color's

STOP

# WRITING/GRAMMAR

**DIRECTIONS**
**Read the passage. Choose the word or words that best fit in each numbered blank. Mark the letter for your answer.**

Dear _____,
    **(1)**
    Thank you for showing me how to make quilt blocks. Yesterday, I _____
                   **(2)**
the third block. Today, I am working on number four. With practice, they are

getting _____ to make. I hope that by the time I see you at Christmas I will
    **(3)**
have twenty finished blocks. Then we can make the quilt top during _____
                   **(4)**

vacation. I can't wait to see what it _____ like when it's done!
       **(5)**
              Love,
              Alison

1  A  Mrs. Clemens
   B  mrs. Clemens
   C  Mrs. clemens
   D  mrs. clemens

2  F  finish
   G  will finish
   H  finishing
   J  finished

3  A  easiest
   B  most easy
   C  more easier
   D  easier

4  F  me
   G  me's
   H  mine
   J  my

5  A  look
   B  looks
   C  looking
   D  looked

GO ON →

# DIRECTIONS

Read the passage and look at the underlined parts. Decide which type of mistake, if any, appears in each underlined part. Mark the letter for your answer.

<u>"Look out Ralph," cried Danny.</u>
**(6)**
"There is a snake by your left foot."

Ralph looked down. "Oh, that."

He picked it up <u>and tossed it at his</u>
**(7)**
<u>buddys feet.</u>

Danny dodged the flying snake,

and Ralph laughed.

<u>"It's just rubber, silly," said</u>
**(8)**
<u>Ralph.</u> "Mom uses them to scare

rodents away from her garden."

6  F  Spelling
   G  Capitalization
   H  Punctuation
   J  No mistake

7  A  Spelling
   B  Capitalization
   C  Punctuation
   D  No mistake

8  F  Spelling
   G  Capitalization
   H  Punctuation
   J  No mistake

GO ON ➤

## DIRECTIONS

Read the passage. Some parts are underlined. The underlined parts may be one of the following:

- **Incomplete sentences**
- **Run-on sentences**
- **Correctly written sentences that should be combined**
- **Correctly written sentences that do not need to be rewritten**

Mark the letter beside the best way to write each underlined part. If the underlined part needs no change, mark the choice "No mistake."

---

In March 1999, Bertrand Piccard and Brian Jones floated around the

world in a hot-air balloon. <u>Took three weeks.</u> When they landed safely, a large
                            **(9)**

crowd was waiting. <u>Although balloonists have tried to circle the globe for</u>
                   **(10)**

<u>hundreds of years. Piccard and Jones were the first to do it.</u>

---

**9 A** Taking three weeks.

　**B** The trip took three weeks.

　**C** Three weeks for the trip.

　**D** No mistake

**10 F** Although balloonists have tried to circle the globe for hundreds of years, and Piccard and Jones were the first to do it.

　**G** Although balloonists have tried to circle the globe for hundreds of years, Piccard and Jones were the first to do it.

　**H** Balloonists have tried to circle the globe for hundreds of years Piccard and Jones were the first to do it.

　**J** No mistake

# WRITING

Think about how you get ready to go to school on weekday mornings.

Write a how-to report that describes how to prepare for school. Be sure to list the steps in a clear and logical way.

**Prewriting Notes**

GO ON

# STUDY SKILLS

**DIRECTIONS**

**Sam is interested in long-distance running. He plans to write a report about the Tarahumara, a native people from Mexico who are known for their running. He begins by looking at a book about the Tarahumara. Use the table of contents and part of the index from the book to answer questions 1–2.**

**Contents**

Introduction . . . . . . . . . . . . . . . 5
1. Geography of the Sierra
   Madre. . . . . . . . . . . . . . . . . 7
2. Isolation from Others . . . . . . 13
3. Government . . . . . . . . . . . . . 25
4. Daily Life. . . . . . . . . . . . . . 37
5. Mountain Runners . . . . . . . 57
Bibliography. . . . . . . . . . . . . . 65
Glossary. . . . . . . . . . . . . . . . 67
Index . . . . . . . . . . . . . . . . . . 69

**Index**

Epidemic. *See* Disease
Farming, 37-43
Fertilizer, 38
Fishing, 12, 40
Footraces, 41, 48, 57-64;
    distance, 57; racecourse, 58;
    races for women, 62-63;
    treatment of runners, 64
Footwear, 57
Housing. *See* Adobe dwellings

1 In which chapter of the book should Sam look for information about the geography of the region in which Tarahumara live?

A Chapter 1

B Chapter 2

C Chapter 3

D Chapter 7

2 On what page will Sam find information about what the Tarahumara wear on their feet when they run?

F page 41

G page 57

H page 58

J page 64

GO ON

# DIRECTIONS

**Sam reads some words he does not know. He looks in a dictionary. Use this part of a dictionary page below to answer questions 3–4.**

## tapir ■ taste

**ta·pir** (tā′pər), *n.* any of several large mammals of tropical America and southern Asia, with hoofs and flexible snouts. Tapirs resemble pigs but are related to horses and rhinoceroses. ❑ *n., pl.* **ta·pir** or **ta·pirs.** ■ Another word that sounds like this is **taper.**

**tap·root** (tap′rüt′), *n.* a main root growing downward.

**taps** (taps), *n.sing. or pl.* signal on a bugle or drum to put out lights at night. Taps is also sounded at military funerals.

**tar**¹ (tär), **1** *n.* a thick, black, sticky substance obtained by the distillation of wood or coal. Tar is used to cover and patch roads, roofs, etc. **2** *v.* to cover with tar: *tar a roof.* **3** *n.* the brownish black residue from the smoke of cigarettes, cigars, etc., containing by-products produced by the burning of tobacco. ❑ *v.* **tarred, tar·ring.** —**tar′like′,** *adj.*

**tar and feather,** to pour heated tar on and cover with feathers as a punishment.

**tar**² (tär), *n.* sailor.

**ta·ra·ma·sa·la·ta** (tä′rä mä sä-lä′tä), *n.* a Greek spread made of olive oil, fish roe, lemon juice, and bread crumbs or mashed potatoes. ❑ *n., pl.* **ta·ra·ma·sa·la·tas.**

**tar·an·tel·la** (tar′ən tel′ə), *n.* **1** a rapid, whirling southern Italian dance with a very quick rhythm. **2** music for this dance ❑ *n., pl.* **tar·an·tel·las.** [See Word Story at tarantula.]

**ta·ran·tu·la** (tə ran′chə lə), *n.* **1** any of various large, hairy spiders living in warm regions, with a painful but usually not serious bite. **2** a large spider of southern Europe with a slightly poisonous bite. ❑ *n., pl.* **ta·ran·tu·las.**

**tarantula** (def. 2)—up to 2 in. (5 cm) long

**3** What is a tarantella?

  **A** a large mammal

  **B** a spider

  **C** a signal on a bugle or drum

  **D** a dance

**4** Which of these words could also appear on this same page of the dictionary?

  **F** tacky

  **G** tax

  **H** tamper

  **J** tarragon

GO ON ▶

# STUDY SKILLS

**DIRECTIONS**

Sam is looking for books about the peoples of Mexico.
When he searches the library database, this screen appears.
Use the screen to help answer questions 5–8.

| Subject: Titles | Call Number |
|---|---|
| **Mexico:** | |
| 1) Mexico and Its History | 921.4 |
| 2) Traveling to Mexico | 975.6 |
| 3) Pablo's Adventure | LOP |
| 4) Mexico: Land of Many Cultures | 934.2 |

Type a number to find out more about a title.
Type A, T, or S to begin a new search.

**5** This screen shows the results of a search by —
  A author.
  B title.
  C subject.
  D call number.

**6** Which book would probably be most useful for Sam's report?
  F *Mexico and Its History*
  G *Traveling to Mexico*
  H *Pablo's Adventure*
  J *Mexico: Land of Many Cultures*

**7** What is the call number for *Traveling to Mexico?*
  A 921.4
  B 975.6
  C LOP
  D 934.2

**8** To find out if the information in a book is up to date, Sam should look at the —
  F copyright page.
  G table of contents.
  H index.
  J cover of the book.

**DIRECTIONS**

Sam found this chart in a textbook. Use the chart to answer questions 9–10.

## Some of the Healthiest People Around the World

| People | Location | Exercise | Diet |
|---|---|---|---|
| Tarahumara | Sierra Madre, Mexico | Long-distance running | 75 percent corn; lots of beans; low-fat diet |
| Masai | Kenya; Tanzania | Walking 10-12 miles per day with cattle | Meat and milk |
| Inuit | Greenland | Hunting | Rich seafood |
| Mormons | Utah, U.S.A. | Various activities | Lots of meat, fruit, and vegetables |

9  According to the chart, what do the Tarahumara eat most?

   **A**  corn and beans

   **B**  rich seafood

   **C**  lots of meat

   **D**  fruit and milk

10  What is the main form of exercise for the Inuit?

   **F**  running

   **G**  walking

   **H**  hunting

   **J**  farming

STOP

# ANSWER SHEET: UNIT SKILLS TEST

Student Name _____ Unit _____

Teacher Name _____ Date _____

**Directions:** Fill in the bubble that matches the number of the test item. In some tests you will not fill in all the bubbles.

## READING:
### Comprehension/Word Analysis

1. Ⓐ Ⓑ Ⓒ Ⓓ
2. Ⓕ Ⓖ Ⓗ Ⓙ
3. Ⓐ Ⓑ Ⓒ Ⓓ
4. Ⓕ Ⓖ Ⓗ Ⓙ
5. Ⓐ Ⓑ Ⓒ Ⓓ
6. Ⓕ Ⓖ Ⓗ Ⓙ
7. Ⓐ Ⓑ Ⓒ Ⓓ
8. Ⓕ Ⓖ Ⓗ Ⓙ
9. Ⓐ Ⓑ Ⓒ Ⓓ
10. Ⓕ Ⓖ Ⓗ Ⓙ
11. Ⓐ Ⓑ Ⓒ Ⓓ
12. Ⓕ Ⓖ Ⓗ Ⓙ
13. Ⓐ Ⓑ Ⓒ Ⓓ
14. Ⓕ Ⓖ Ⓗ Ⓙ
15. Ⓐ Ⓑ Ⓒ Ⓓ
16. Ⓕ Ⓖ Ⓗ Ⓙ
17. Ⓐ Ⓑ Ⓒ Ⓓ
18. Ⓕ Ⓖ Ⓗ Ⓙ
19. Ⓐ Ⓑ Ⓒ Ⓓ
20. Ⓕ Ⓖ Ⓗ Ⓙ
21. Ⓐ Ⓑ Ⓒ Ⓓ
22. Ⓕ Ⓖ Ⓗ Ⓙ
23. Ⓐ Ⓑ Ⓒ Ⓓ
24. Ⓕ Ⓖ Ⓗ Ⓙ
25. Ⓐ Ⓑ Ⓒ Ⓓ
26. Ⓕ Ⓖ Ⓗ Ⓙ
27. Ⓐ Ⓑ Ⓒ Ⓓ
28. Ⓕ Ⓖ Ⓗ Ⓙ
29. Ⓐ Ⓑ Ⓒ Ⓓ
30. Ⓕ Ⓖ Ⓗ Ⓙ

## WRITING/GRAMMAR

1. Ⓐ Ⓑ Ⓒ Ⓓ
2. Ⓕ Ⓖ Ⓗ Ⓙ
3. Ⓐ Ⓑ Ⓒ Ⓓ
4. Ⓕ Ⓖ Ⓗ Ⓙ
5. Ⓐ Ⓑ Ⓒ Ⓓ
6. Ⓕ Ⓖ Ⓗ Ⓙ

## STUDY SKILLS

1. Ⓐ Ⓑ Ⓒ Ⓓ
2. Ⓕ Ⓖ Ⓗ Ⓙ
3. Ⓐ Ⓑ Ⓒ Ⓓ
4. Ⓕ Ⓖ Ⓗ Ⓙ
5. Ⓐ Ⓑ Ⓒ Ⓓ
6. Ⓕ Ⓖ Ⓗ Ⓙ
7. Ⓐ Ⓑ Ⓒ Ⓓ
8. Ⓕ Ⓖ Ⓗ Ⓙ
9. Ⓐ Ⓑ Ⓒ Ⓓ
10. Ⓕ Ⓖ Ⓗ Ⓙ

# ANSWER SHEET: END-OF-YEAR SKILLS TEST

Student Name _____ Unit _____

Teacher Name _____ Date _____

**Directions:** Fill in the bubble that matches the number of the test item.

## READING: Comprehension

1. (A) (B) (C) (D)
2. (F) (G) (H) (J)
3. (A) (B) (C) (D)
4. (F) (G) (H) (J)
5. (A) (B) (C) (D)
6. (F) (G) (H) (J)
7. (A) (B) (C) (D)
8. (F) (G) (H) (J)
9. (A) (B) (C) (D)
10. (F) (G) (H) (J)
11. (A) (B) (C) (D)
12. (F) (G) (H) (J)
13. (A) (B) (C) (D)
14. (F) (G) (H) (J)
15. (A) (B) (C) (D)
16. (F) (G) (H) (J)
17. (A) (B) (C) (D)
18. (F) (G) (H) (J)
19. (A) (B) (C) (D)
20. (F) (G) (H) (J)
21. (A) (B) (C) (D)
22. (F) (G) (H) (J)
23. (A) (B) (C) (D)
24. (F) (G) (H) (J)
25. (A) (B) (C) (D)
26. (F) (G) (H) (J)
27. (A) (B) (C) (D)
28. (F) (G) (H) (J)
29. (A) (B) (C) (D)
30. (F) (G) (H) (J)

## READING: Word Analysis

1. (A) (B) (C) (D)
2. (F) (G) (H) (J)
3. (A) (B) (C) (D)
4. (F) (G) (H) (J)
5. (A) (B) (C) (D)
6. (F) (G) (H) (J)
7. (A) (B) (C) (D)
8. (F) (G) (H) (J)
9. (A) (B) (C) (D)
10. (F) (G) (H) (J)

## WRITING/GRAMMAR

1. (A) (B) (C) (D)
2. (F) (G) (H) (J)
3. (A) (B) (C) (D)
4. (F) (G) (H) (J)
5. (A) (B) (C) (D)
6. (F) (G) (H) (J)
7. (A) (B) (C) (D)
8. (F) (G) (H) (J)
9. (A) (B) (C) (D)
10. (F) (G) (H) (J)

## STUDY SKILLS

1. (A) (B) (C) (D)
2. (F) (G) (H) (J)
3. (A) (B) (C) (D)
4. (F) (G) (H) (J)
5. (A) (B) (C) (D)
6. (F) (G) (H) (J)
7. (A) (B) (C) (D)
8. (F) (G) (H) (J)
9. (A) (B) (C) (D)
10. (F) (G) (H) (J)

# ANSWER KEY

## Unit 1 Skills Test

### READING: Comprehension

1. B
2. H
3. C
4. J
5. A
6. H
7. C
8. F
9. D
10. G
11. C
12. F
13. B
14. J
15. A
16. H
17. A
18. H
19. C
20. G
21. A
22. J
23. B
24. J
25. D

### WRITING/GRAMMAR

1. C
2. J
3. C
4. F
5. B

### WRITING

### Scoring Guide: Personal Narrative

**4 Exemplary**
- Flows from beginning to middle to end
- Rich use of detail reveals writer's feelings.
- Keen sense of audience and purpose
- Vivid word choice reveals writer's voice.
- Errors do not prevent understanding.

**3 Competent**
- Clear beginning, middle, end
- Details reveal writer's feelings
- Sense of audience and purpose
- Word choice reveals writer's voice.
- Errors do not prevent understanding.

**2 Developing**
- Lacks clear beginning, middle, and end
- A few details suggest feelings.
- Lacks clear sense of audience and purpose
- Limited or vague word choice
- Errors may prevent understanding.

**1 Emerging**
- No movement from beginning to end
- Writer fails to reveal self through details.
- No sense of audience and purpose
- Incorrect or redundant word choice
- Errors prevent understanding.

### STUDY SKILLS

1. A
2. G
3. C
4. G
5. B
6. F
7. D
8. G
9. C
10. H

# ANSWER KEY

## Unit 2 Skills Test

### READING: Comprehension

1. B
2. F
3. D
4. J
5. C
6. J
7. B
8. F
9. D
10. H
11. D
12. G
13. B
14. F
15. C
16. J
17. A
18. H
19. B
20. F
21. C
22. J
23. A
24. G

### WRITING/GRAMMAR

1. B
2. H
3. A
4. J
5. B
6. F

## WRITING

### Scoring Guide: Description

**4 Exemplary**
- Vivid sense words and images
- Ideas clear and focused
- Elaboration with strong details
- Clear, varied, smooth sentences
- Errors do not prevent understanding.

**3 Competent**
- Includes sense words and images
- Ideas generally clear and focused
- Elaboration with three or more details
- Most sentences varied and smooth
- Errors do not prevent understanding.

**2 Developing**
- Some sense words; images may not be clear
- Ideas may lack focus and clarity.
- Elaboration with two or more details
- Simple sentences; sometimes awkward
- Errors may prevent understanding.

**1 Emerging**
- Few or no sense words or images
- Ideas lack focus and clarity.
- Lacks elaboration
- Incomplete and/or awkward sentences
- Errors prevent understanding.

## STUDY SKILLS

1. A
2. J
3. B
4. F
5. B
6. J
7. C
8. G
9. A
10. H

## Unit 3 Skills Test

### READING: Comprehension

1. D
2. H
3. A
4. G
5. B
6. J
7. A
8. H
9. D
10. F
11. B
12. J
13. C
14. H
15. D
16. F
17. B
18. J
19. A
20. F
21. B
22. J
23. C
24. F

### READING: Word Analysis

25. D
26. H
27. A
28. J
29. C
30. J

### WRITING/GRAMMAR

1. B
2. J
3. C
4. J
5. A

## WRITING

### Scoring Guide: Comparison/Contrast Essay

**4 Exemplary**
- Clear topic sentence
- Ideas are organized and flow smoothly.
- Transitions show likenesses and differences.
- Clear, varied, smooth sentences
- Errors do not prevent understanding.

**3 Competent**
- Understandable topic sentence
- Ideas generally organized
- Some transitions
- Most sentences varied and smooth
- Errors do not prevent understanding.

**2 Developing**
- Attempts to write a topic sentence
- Some ideas seem unconnected
- Could use more transitions
- Simple sentences; sometimes awkward
- Errors may prevent understanding.

**1 Emerging**
- No topic sentence
- Ideas seem unconnected.
- Few or no transitions
- Incomplete and/or awkward sentences
- Errors prevent understanding.

### STUDY SKILLS

1. C
2. J
3. B
4. F
5. B

# ANSWER KEY

## Unit 4 Skills Test

### READING: Comprehension

1. D
2. H
3. A
4. J
5. C
6. G
7. C
8. J
9. B
10. F
11. A
12. H
13. B
14. H
15. B
16. J
17. A
18. G
19. A
20. H
21. D
22. G
23. C
24. F

### READING: Word Analysis

25. D
26. G
27. A
28. J
29. A
30. G

### WRITING/GRAMMAR

1. C
2. G
3. A
4. F
5. C

## WRITING

### Scoring Guide: How-To Report

**4 Exemplary**
- Task fully defined
- Ample information provided
- Words like *first* indicate order of steps.
- Clear sentences guide reader.
- Errors do not prevent understanding.

**3 Competent**
- Task defined
- Adequate information provided
- Words like *first* indicate order of steps.
- Sentences are generally clear.
- Errors do not prevent understanding.

**2 Developing**
- Limited definition of task
- May have gaps in information
- Needs more words to show order of steps
- Sentences could be clearer.
- Errors may prevent understanding.

**1 Emerging**
- No attempt to define task
- Inadequate information provided
- No words used to show order of steps.
- Sentences lack clarity and confuse reader.
- Errors prevent understanding.

## STUDY SKILLS

1. B
2. J
3. C
4. J
5. B
6. H
7. B
8. G
9. C
10. G

# ANSWER KEY

## Unit 5 Skills Test

### READING: Comprehension

1. A
2. H
3. B
4. H
5. D
6. G
7. B
8. F
9. C
10. G
11. A
12. G
13. B
14. F
15. B
16. J
17. D
18. G
19. B
20. H
21. C
22. F
23. B
24. J

### READING: Word Analysis

25. D
26. F
27. C
28. F
29. A
30. H

### WRITING/GRAMMAR

1. A
2. F
3. C
4. H
5. B

### WRITING

### Scoring Guide: Research Report

**4 Exemplary**
- Strong introduction and conclusion
- Information complete and well organized
- Good use of source
- Clear, varied, smooth sentences
- Errors do not prevent understanding.

**3 Competent**
- Good introduction and conclusion
- Information complete and organized
- Good use of source
- Most sentences varied and smooth
- Errors do not prevent understanding.

**2 Developing**
- Attempts an introduction and conclusion
- May have gaps in information
- Source is not well used.
- Simple sentences; sometimes awkward
- Errors may prevent understanding.

**1 Emerging**
- No introduction and conclusion
- Inadequate information provided
- Source is not well used.
- Incomplete and/or awkward sentences
- Errors prevent understanding.

### STUDY SKILLS

1. B
2. F
3. D
4. H
5. D

# ANSWER KEY

## Unit 6 Skills Test

### READING: Comprehension

1. B
2. G
3. C
4. F
5. C
6. J
7. A
8. J
9. D
10. F
11. C
12. H
13. D
14. G
15. A
16. H
17. D
18. J
19. A
20. F
21. C
22. J
23. B
24. G

### READING: Word Analysis

25. D
26. H
27. A
28. G
29. C
30. J

### WRITING/GRAMMAR

1. B
2. H
3. C
4. J
5. A

## WRITING

### Scoring Guide: Persuasive Argument

**4 Exemplary**
- Clear issues and writer's opinion
- Convincing details and evidence
- Distinctive voice and vivid word choice
- Vivid word choice reveals writer's voice.
- Errors do not prevent understanding.

**3 Competent**
- Shows issues and writer's opinion
- Supporting details and evidence
- Voice shown in word choice
- Errors do not prevent understanding.

**2 Developing**
- Issues and opinions may lack clarity.
- Some supporting details and evidence
- Writer's voice weak; vague word choice
- Errors may prevent understanding.

**1 Emerging**
- Undeveloped issues and opinions
- Weak supporting details and evidence
- No clear voice; incorrect word choice
- Errors prevent understanding.

## STUDY SKILLS

1. A
2. J
3. B
4. J
5. A

# ANSWER KEY

## End-of-Year Skills Test

### READING: Comprehension

1. B
2. J
3. C
4. F
5. D
6. J
7. B
8. J
9. D
10. F
11. B
12. J
13. B
14. F
15. C
16. H
17. B
18. F
19. D
20. F
21. D
22. G
23. A
24. J
25. C

### READING: Word Analysis

1. A
2. H
3. D
4. G
5. C
6. J
7. A
8. F
9. B
10. H

### WRITING/GRAMMAR

1. A
2. J
3. D
4. J
5. B

6. H
7. C
8. J
9. B
10. G

## WRITING

### Scoring Guide: How-To Report

**4 Exemplary**
- Task fully defined
- Ample information provided
- Words like *first* indicate order of steps.
- Clear sentences guide reader.
- Errors do not prevent understanding.

**3 Competent**
- Task defined
- Adequate information provided
- Words such as *first* indicate order of steps.
- Sentences are generally clear.
- Errors do not prevent understanding.

**2 Developing**
- Limited definition of task
- May have gaps in information
- Needs more words to show order of steps
- Sentences could be clearer.
- Errors may prevent understanding.

**1 Emerging**
- No attempt to define task
- Inadequate information provided
- No words used to show order of steps.
- Sentences lack clarity and confuse reader.
- Errors prevent understanding.

## STUDY SKILLS

1. A
2. G
3. D
4. J
5. C
6. J
7. B
8. F
9. A
10. H